TAKE OFF FROM WITHIN

T0151842

TAKE OFF FROM WITHIN
by Ervin Seale

DeVorss Publications

Take Off from Within
Copyright © 1971 by Ervin Seale

Library of Congress Catalog Card Number: 71-150974
ISBN: 978-087516-658-2
Third Printing, 2023

DeVorss & Company, Publisher
PO Box 1389
Camarillo CA 93011-1389
www.devorss.com
Printed in the United States of America

Contents

Foreword

There is an ancient mind principle which will get anyone out of difficulty and help him into any desirable good. It is a kind of open secret—as obvious as the fact that a person has hands and feet, as obscure as the undiscovered ability of a child who has not yet discovered the use of his limbs.

This book is meant as a reminder of that ancient mind principle and its application to the common situations of everyday life. The book has but one thing to say but tries to say it in a variety of ways.

If it is true that as a man thinks so is he, then thinking is the most consequential activity of a human being. In these pages I have tried to recall to mind and present anew some of the tools of the trade whereby one may become a better craftsman in the production of health and happiness.

This book is not religious; it is spiritual. It does not talk about religion but about the spirit of man and the mind which directs that spirit. It tries to avoid telling anyone what to think; rather, it tries to tell a person how to think.

I am greatly indebted to many people who have helped me to put these words together but chiefly to my wife, Elva, who freed me of other tasks to enable me to do this; to my long-time friend and co-worker, Elsa Thern who set aside her own concerns to put my dictation into typescript, to Christine Wier for initial help with the typing, and to Annabel Learned for invaluable editorial help with the manuscript.

ERVIN SEALE

The Great Mind Principle

Examine the stream of your thoughts and notice how many of them are about the regretted past and the uncertain future. A thousand advisers have told us to learn to live in the present, but very few of us do. This book will give some hints about living in the present. Actually, we are always living in the present moment—we can do no other. When we worry about the future or look back in remorse at the past, it is in the present that we do it. The past is simply old scenes brought into present consciousness. The future is today's concern with what is unknowable. What you think now of the past and the future are present thoughts, and only present thought determines whether you are happy or miserable.

Consciousness is a spot of light between two darknesses. All a man is is what he knows, as that spot of light moves from experience to experience and from event to event. Distressing or pleasing, it makes no difference whether he thinks of the past or of the future: either way, it is really the present. In dreamless sleep there is neither past nor future. Whatever troublesome event may be taking place while one sleeps, it cannot affect him until he wakes to know it. Your real life is the present moment. That is all you have to deal with, all you can deal with.

This is why the past and the future are the storied thieves of health and happiness. They rob the present of its vitality, effectiveness, and peace. Shuttling between yesterday and tomorrow, the mind loses force in the present and hangs suspended, incapable of forward motion. It is thus crucified, hung up, immobilized, and dies between the thieves, one of which (the past) wails and mocks and the other (the future) begs a boon when life returns, as it must and will (Luke 22).

When life returns to the troubled mind, it comes in the realization that it is itself arbiter of past and future and all things besides. Consciousness alone is real. The past is dead except as memory revives it. The future is only such life as present thought conceives and nurtures. The return of health and vigor to the mind and person come in the awareness that we never have anything to deal with, in either worry or praise, but our thoughts. We cannot deal directly with the past or with the future—they are untouchable to us. We can only think about our concepts of them and what pleases or displeases us; in that moment of pleasure or displeasure is our life and our only life. Whatever the past is in itself, to us it is only today's thought. Whatever the future may be, to us it is only what we think today.

Therefore "Look to this day, for it is the very life of life. In its brief course lie all the verities and realities of your existence." Learn to live one day at a time. Learn to manage this hour, this minute, for it is all you have. Yet it is enough. Handle this minute well and you can redeem the past and insure the future.

Whenever you are troubled or sore beset by any difficulty, don't fight the problem and go around and around the annoying details. Rather, retire within yourself and achieve a harmony and an equanimity based upon the knowledge that it is not what happens to you *but what you think about what happens to you* that makes the difference between happiness and misery, success and failure, health and illness. Get this principle firmly in mind now, for it is the heart of what we have to say in these pages and the cardinal principle of sovereignty for man. Not people or events, but the beholding mind, is the sovereign agent in all human experience. See this until you no longer debate the point. Understand it until it becomes an absolute with you, and then you will have power—you will not give your power away to people and events and things. In every distressing situation, as soon as the mind retires within itself and anchors itself to a few principles like this and returns to equanimity and harmony, it has the distressing situation within its power.

When Ignatius Loyola heard the news that an unfriendly man had been elected pope, he was asked what he would do if the new head of the Church should order the Society of Jesus dissolved, the work in which Loyola had invested his life, he replied, "Fifteen minutes in orison and all will be the same." What did he mean? How can it be the same if all you have put your heart into is destroyed in a single hour? What can you do in orison to make it right?

You can remember the sovereignty of mind and spirit and the subserviency of things and conditions. Do you doubt this? Then bring forth your other theories and marshal the evidence to support them. Are things and conditions in the saddle? Is matter more than mind? Does one condition make another condition? Are the experiences of human beings determined by things outside of them or by ideation within them? Is there any one sovereign, initiating force in life, or are we all the victims of chance and blind fate?

If you can settle the debate in your mind on this point, then you return to the strong assurance that no condition or event can mar your course, or even the election of an unfriendly pope. Fifteen minutes in orison have changed the face of fear.

Said Professor Max Mueller, "It is one of the most remarkable aberrations of the human mind that it thinks there can be

a word without a thought or a thought without a word"* This
is because there is little general understanding of the great
truth that humans most often try to manage their condition
without prior management of their thought. Word is the expression of thought, not only in speech and in writing but in
action. When Emerson says, "What you are, preaches so
loudly I cannot hear what you say," he is observing that a
person's action is the real expression of his inmost thought—
conscious or subconscious or both. Knowledge of this great
fundamental principle of the mind always brings deliverance,
and ignorance of it misery. The Bible speaks of these two as
the Father and the Son, for the Father is the thought or the
cause and the Son is the expression. They are inseparable but
they can be distinguished. Because they are inseparable, a man
"shall give account of every idle word in the day of judgment." Not at some far-off time when "the roll is called up
yonder," but at any time when a person's thought is full and
complete along a certain line, then is the time of judgment or
the coming of the word to expression.

People sometimes object to this philosophy of cause and
effect, saying perhaps, "You talk about the law of thought and
how we are what we think and how we get what we think
and so on, but I wasn't thinking of a cold and look at the
whopper I got!"

Another will say, "I wasn't thinking of an accident, and look
at this awful thing that happened to me." But much thinking
goes on subconsciously. It is sufficient only to be nervous to
have an accident. It is sufficient only to be tired to "catch" a
heavy cold. Much of our thinking goes on unwittingly at the
involuntary level. Many ridiculous and negative ideas enter
the mind at this level, and the conscious mind is for the most
part unaware of them until they come to expression. No person of insight will ever deny that his expression is the result
of his thought, even though he was not previously aware of

---

* *Thoughts on Life and Religion* (New York: E. P. Dutton & Co., 1905), p. 13.

it. Things build up in the subconscious until there is a day of reckoning or judgment, a day when the thought comes to expression—as the Bible puts it, "When the moon is full."

Ordinarily we do not like to believe that thought and word, cause and effect, are one: that the Father is in us, and that the Father is thought. The Father is thought or mind or consciousness, and every thought fathers a word or an expression. We commonly think of word as meaning a vocalization, or some sound from the lips or letters on a page such as you are reading now. But these are only symbols of the word. The true word is the thought in the mind and heart, and by extension, the gesture of the hand or movement of the body, or the experience of the whole person, whether in extremity or in joy and happiness. This is the great Mind Principle, and when one is ready to take the responsibility upon himself that every expression in his world is the result of his own thought, voluntary or involuntary, then he is ready to make the great Mind Principle work for him instead of against him.

It is true that very often when a person first comes to this realization and gets rid of the aberration that there can be a thought without a word, he is afraid. He becomes fearful of his own thought and what is in store for him because of it. But as his realization clarifies further he comes to jubilation, for since there is an unconditional contract between thought and word, he is equipped and regnant and free, and there is no outside power compelling him. He can think his own gracious, beautiful, constructive thoughts and allow the Father principle within to bring them into manifestation.

In this great Mind Principle of the Father and the Son or Thought and Word is found a peculiar blending of Greek and Hebrew background. The Hebrew said that the name of God is I AM (mind, awareness, presence, consciousness). The Greek said that thought (the local action of Universal Mind) is expressed as word. The Greek name for both thought and word was *logos,* by which he indicated the inner and the outer of the same thing, distinguishable but inseparable. The most

profound, revolutionary, life-changing truth is involved in this
concept. It is empowering and enfranchising. It gives a basis
for faith—not faith in something or someone outside of man,
but faith through rational insight into the great Mind Principle
that governs all human experience.

When Moses stood before the burning bush and contem-
plated the mystery of matter all aflame and illumined, yet not
consumed, the realization was born that matter is first of all
mind-stuff—or, as modern science shows, all matter is made
up of particles of light or energy. The voice from the burning
bush announced, "Put off thy shoes from off thy feet, for the
place whereon thou standest is holy ground." That is, take off
the coverings of your understanding, those opinions and pre-
conditioned viewpoints and prejudices which come between
you and the pure ground of your being. The feet are what we
stand on, physically and literally. They are our support. But
since there is an inner and an outer meaning to all things, the
feet become the symbol or representative of the inner sup-
ports of our life: our understanding and our insight and attitudes.

Where do you stand? On what do you stand? Do you have
an insight such as this great Mind Principle which, whenever
you think of it, refreshes you, encourages you, and stabilizes
and harmonizes you? If so, you have something to stand on
when the winds and waves of worldly thought and human
emotion assail you. Human opinions and fears and prejudices
which we inherit from the racial or worldly mind tend to
surround and inhibit the tremendous creative power within
us. Thus the direction is: Take the coverings off and let your
bare feet come down upon this holy ground of universal being
which is your source and your life. Let that speak to you which
has no second and knows no other, and which says, "My glory
will I not give to another . . . Is there a God beside me? Yea,
there is no God; I know not any" (Isa. 42, 44).

Notice the absoluteness of this statement. Universal Mind
has the glory of being the primal and only source and cause

of all things and expressions, and it has no rival. Mathematically, it could not have. For where there are two, there is the possibility of friction and antagonism. If there were two Creators there would be no cosmos, only chaos. That is why the ancient Jew harps on the theme, "Hear, O Israel, the Lord thy God is one Lord." There is one and only one creative power, and it is mind or consciousness.

The same absoluteness must come to the individual mind which is simply an operating center of Universal Mind, operating on a smaller scale, if it is to have power and not be moved about willy-nilly, in ignorance, by the phenomenal world. Mind, consciousness, thought, is the only *making* power. Therefore deal with the cause and not with the effect.

To this tremendous revelation of the Hebrew, the Greek added his practical turn of thought and showed that all thought is the divine or local action of the Universal Mind. Thus the mind that made the universe and the mind that thinks in a human being are one, though they work at different levels. But thought is thought and always creative; it always results in its expressed word. It is the God power whether at the universal or individual level of being.

Thus, Jesus is called the Word of God because he is the portrayal of the type of man who fully expresses the universal as individualized being. He shows us the Father. In nearly all religions, God remains far from man, but not in the religion of Jesus. When Philip asks Jesus, "Show us the Father," he replies, "Have I been so long time with you, and yet hast thou not known me, Philip? he that hath seen me hath seen the Father" (John 14:9). That is, he who understands (sees) man understands (sees) God. Every man is some expression of God. Jesus is the portrayal of the full expression.

The same principle holds true at the local level: every act, gesture, or experience in one's personal life is the expression of a constellation of thoughts in the mind which is the father of the expression. There can be no act without a thought and no thought without an act. In the beginning of every event is the word, and the word is God or the making power or moving cause, or unseen creative force. He who sees my body, sees my thought. He who sees my actions sees my consciousness. We cannot perceive thought except as and in its expression. Therefore, he that hath seen me hath seen the Father. All that we do in a visible way is the result of our invisible mode of thought.

Gibran says it constructively and poetically when he remarks that, "work is love made visible."* Real work is love made visible, but sometimes our work is drudgery and toil, and then it is our drudgery and toil that become visible instead of our love. Sometimes we work with a bitter heart. Gibran says, "If you bake bread with a bitter heart, you make a bitter loaf that feeds but half man's hunger." Whatever we do with a bitter heart becomes a bitter thing. All this is not mere poetry. It is science. It is law. As soon as a person hears it with insight, it becomes his personal law and he is ready for the life-changing act. From knowing that all his activity and all his expression and experience are his word or his thought made visible, two things will happen to him.

First, he will no longer fear things and expressions and conditions and people and circumstances and events as he formerly did. They will become for him what they have always really been: mere objects, and his attitude will be objective and not emotional. Then, he will understand anew the old instruction, "Fear not them which kill the body, but are not able to kill the soul: but rather fear him which is able to destroy both soul and body in hell" (Matt. 10).

Physical things can mar and kill other physical things, but only secondarily. Physical things are governed and directed by metaphysical things, and if the metaphysical things are handled correctly and kept harmonious, the physical things cannot act except in obedience to the metaphysical. If the mind in ignorance gives away its power to physical things and believes

* *The Prophet.*

that they are self-acting, then it empties its receptacle—which was filled with power—and, nothing being there, the vacuum is known as fear and anxiety and all the host of corrosive emotions associated with them.

Then the soul which would move forward by its natural desires and impulses finds itself locked by its fear of an opposing force. The result is friction, and friction is heat, and this is the fabled hell-fire so literalized by preachers of a former day. When mind and soul burn in their own internal turmoil, then the body is not far from destruction. But take care of the primary part and the secondary part will take care of itself.

The ancients called spirit and soul and mind "the better part"—not because the body was considered mean and earthy, but because the mind is primary. The body is a bag of earth, but a glorious one, ingeniously and exquisitely arranged to portray and re-present the invisible nature of the soul. The body is not less important than the soul, but it is secondary and follows after. As biology teaches, function precedes organism. When the phenomenal world intrudes too much on consciousness and threatens or obstructs, the discerning mind will retire within, reminding itself of these rudimentary principles, and come again to peace and harmony and balance and equanimity. Then it is sovereign, the Lord is in his holy temple, and every stick and stone is in loyal and harmonious obedience to the Law or Lord within.

This, then, is the first step of the mind that discerns and beholds the great Mind Principle. It frees itself from the tyranny of events and things and people and conditions. It no longer puts fear into externals. It no longer gives its power away. It is born of God and does not commit sin, for its seed remaineth in it (1 John 3). To recover this sovereign position of mind and spirit is the office of prayer, meditation, right thinking, and orison.

The second step that the mind which discerns this principle will take is that it will gradually but firmly squelch the strong temptation in all humans to talk about their troubles, their aches and pains, and to describe illness and bad luck and the folly and foolishness of men in general. Such a mind will curb the tendency to condemn or resent, and the strong urge to describe people and conditions in any other fashion than as the person himself would have them be. He will learn to keep the Golden Rule, not as a moral preachment but as a science. He will do unto others as he would be done by, not only in outer acts of honesty and fair dealing but in inward acts of attitude, concept, and estimation.

Essentially, the Golden Rule is a rule not for external conduct but for thinking. When a person correctly estimates himself, he will respect himself, and his respect will be projected as a natural consequence to all other men and indeed to all living things. Love your neighbor as yourself. If you do not love yourself, you cannot possibly love others. The inhumanity of man to man can be explained on no other basis. Prejudice has been defined as "being down on something you're not up on." If you are up on yourself, you are also up on others. If you understand that all men are wayfarers on the way to self-discovery, you will not be incensed that some men live beneath themselves, including yourself sometimes. Your charity and generosity of attitude will flow in sympathy and empathy, and you will prosper even as your soul prospers. Other men are not our enemies. Things and conditions are not obstructive of the soul's true impulses and desires. There is no antagonist but the thought of one.

The countless crimes and offenses of individual to individual, nation to nation, and race to race all stem from men's inward crimes against themselves. The discerning mind will first of all have a kindness for itself, and then it cannot be unkind to anyone either in thought or in act. Those who labor at solutions in the parliaments of the world could do no better than to return to this ancient landmark which our fathers have set, and those who seek the benefits of education will seek the greatest good in vain until this ancient rule is taught again and

taught clearly. Be careful what you think of others, for your
thinking of others governs you.

A cool and objective assessment of the present facts in any
situation or person is one thing and quite necessary and intelli-
gent, but running a mental movie of the scene over and over
again with full sound is quite another thing and productive
only of harm. Especially people who are ill tend to talk. We
all love sympathy and would like other people to know how
we hurt. A minimum of this is all right within the family; that
is what families are for. But keep any description of trouble
or sickness or error minimal, for there is something inside
which is listening, and it says, "Oh, you like this! I will make
you a lot more of it." Walt Whitman said that he loved the
animals because they suffered in silence. "I think I could turn
and live with the animals. They do not sweat and whine about
their condition, they do not lie awake in the dark and weep
for their sins, they do not make me sick discussing their duty
to God, not one is dissatisfied, not one is demented with the
mania of owning things."* Such self-containment, which
Whitman admired in animals and held as an ideal for men, can
be had only when one has a strong inward philosophical position such as the great Mind Principle provides: there can be
no thing without its thought and no thought without its thing.

We live in two realms, the realm of thought and the realm
of action, and they are inseparable. One may say, "Everything
depends upon my action; I leave my mind alone." He is
deluded. Another says, "If I think right, it matters not how I
act." He is equally deluded. The first is deceived because,
though he may think he leaves his mind alone, it is never
alone, since the world mind is always in attendance upon the
personal mind. The world mind is always pouring sensations
and impressions upon the personal mind. Ridiculous ideas are
all about us every day, impinging upon the receptive medium
of our personal minds: fear, sickness, loss, war, accidents, and

---

*"Song of Myself" in *Leaves of Grass* (Modern Library Edition, 1921), p. 51.

so on. We take in these impressions without knowing or believing them consciously, and then by repetition we involuntarily believe in the wrong thing and do not know that we believe. We become hooked or hung up on ideas and beliefs not of our own making. We are like a hypnotized man being told that he is weak and not being able consciously to refute the suggestion. He is as weak as he has been told he is.

As Phineas Quimby observed in his original researches, "Man acts as he is acted upon." Superficial thinkers would take this to signify that a man is mean because others have been mean to him, that he is poor because the conditions into which he was born have forced poverty upon him, or sick by inheritance—that we are all victims of our environment. But this is only superficially true. People are mean or poor or sick because of ideas which have been enthroned unwittingly in their minds. Conditions have not done it. The suggestion of conditions has done it. Suggestions from the external world are not powers in and of themselves. They are only suggestions as to how the native and sovereign power of the individual should work.

When Calvin Coolidge was Speaker of the House in Massachusetts, two members got to quarreling and hurling epithets at one another. One rose to such a passion as to consign the other to the hot place. The aggrieved member appealed to the Speaker for an apology. The Speaker considered the request and calmly remarked: "You don't have to go." Indeed, no one has to go where any sensation, impression, or suggestion indicates. Let him remember that he is a free, sovereign soul by nature, and let him be his own suggester and know that his own clear thought, based on true principles, is regnant, divine, and wholly directive of his life.

The person who believes that if he thinks right it does not make any difference how he acts is also in great delusion. No man can live on one side of the equation exclusively. It is a universal will that makes thought and action always equal and compels our motion to equal our emotion. No person can deliberately think right simply because he wishes to do so. For many thoughts are thinking themselves involuntarily within him, and only when he sees through the eyes of a Moses and thinks with the mind of a Greek—only when he stands upon the holy ground and understands the great Mind Principle—does he have a leverage over his thoughts.

These thoughts are from two sources. They are from the sense world around us, as already mentioned, and they are from the Universal or God Mind or the Spirit, this being thought not yet conscious. From this latter source come our inspirations, our desires and urges toward the ideal life. From the environmental side come suggestions of limitation and opposition and weakness and sickness, and from the inspirational side come hope and upreach and outreach. Where these two kinds of thinking meet there is usually conflict, and that is hell. It is God in us that makes us desire to be well, to be healthy, to be happy, to have a place in the sun, and to be satisfied and fulfilled. This is instinctive and inspirational. But in the arena of the human mind it meets with the judgments and opinions and suggestions that come from the material side of life, and then comes the quarrel.

"If I had not come and spoken unto them, they had not had sin: but now they have no cloak for their sin" (John 15). That means that if the Ideal had not come, the mind would know nothing better than its present limited state and there would be no quarrel, therefore no sense of limitation, no misery or sin. But since inspiration has come announcing something better, the trouble is obvious. The mind is torn between two opposites: what one is quarrels with what one would like to be. This is the basic conflict of all human nature and experience. All other conflicts, by whatever name or description, have their source in this.

In closing this chapter, let us apply the great Mind Principle constructively. Every true desire is of God. It is God coming to the individual and asking him to believe in this desire and accept it. Practice to meet the holy visitor with faith.

I have called it a stranger, and indeed it is. "Be not forgetful to entertain strangers: for thereby some have entertained angels unawares" (Heb. 13:2). Intend your mind hospitably toward the visitor. Begin to describe yourself in its terms as free, energetic, healthy, progressive, fulfilled, prosperous, kind, peaceful, loving, efficient, enduring. Your first attempt may be painful. All that you have previously thought will challenge the newcomer. When we did not know the great Mind Principle, we accepted willy-nilly what was spoken into us. Now, knowing the Father as Universal Mind speaking truth and wisdom and courage and strength and peace into us, let us accept it rather than the counterfeit. This is prayer. This is creative thinking. It is right thinking. Let us know that the negative has no power in and of itself to force its ideas upon us. It is we who are the power.

Put Mind In—Take Mind Out

The mind is not only an organ. It is a medium, of ideas and impressions. The mind is a hopper into which impressions fall from two sources, from the external world of the senses and from the internal world of inspiration. What the judgment does with these impressions determines the way we go in life. Intend the mind toward any subject or render it amenable to any series of impressions and it becomes a compulsive force carrying these impressions into functions and consequences.

In an Austrian provincial hospital a man lay dying. The physicians told him they could not diagnose his ailment, but if they could they probably could cure him. There was one hope, however. A famous diagnostician from Vienna was coming to visit the hospital soon, and he could probably diagnose the man's condition. The patient was filled with hope and assurance, and he intended his mind wholeheartedly in the direction of that hope and assurance. The great diagnostician came. As he passed through the wards he read the charts and examined the patients and gave his verdict on each. When he passed this particular man's bed, he gave only a cursory glance and murmured the one word, "Moribundus." But the man lived! He made it his business some time later to call on the great diagnostician. He told him, "I have long wanted to thank you for saving my life. When you passed my bed and murmured that one word, 'Moribundus,' I knew I would get well."*

The more mind one puts into anything, the more it will respond in terms of the quality of the mind that is invested. Put mind into anything and it will flourish. Take mind out of anything and it will wither and depart from consciousness and thence from experience. Knowledge of this principle gives a person sovereignty and control. The impressions that come to his mind are not directly under his control, but his judgment is. It is not what happens to us or around us that determines our life's course, but rather our opinion of what happens. This opinion is within our control, and nothing and no one can divest us of this regnancy in life.

A few years ago in the city of New York the papers recorded the death of a Bowery bum. But he was more than a Bowery bum. He had been a professor of English at a college for women. Handsome, cultured, and urbane, he had been lionized by the girls of the school and generally loved by all who knew him. Why, then, did he take to alcohol to drown whatever secret sorrow ate at his heart and destroyed his will for constructive living? The papers provided an answer in his own words from an interview by a reporter a year or so before his death: "I loved too much the sad poetry and the sad songs."

All too few of us have learned to love ourselves, and that is why we find it so difficult to love our neighbor. The moral imperative of both Moses and Jesus is clear: "Love your neighbor *as* you love yourself." But how to do it is not always clear, though the directions are written down. Many have rejected themselves and even hate themselves, and this self-hate is

---

*Gordon W. Allport, in *Journal of Religion and Health*, 4:1 (October 1964).

projected onto others. From this single cause come more of the world's inhumanities and wars than from any other source. One can never love himself as he ought until he esteems himself in terms of his spiritual heritage—a divinely generated being, destined to win, to achieve, and to express the nature of his source. As water rises no higher than the level of its source, so a man can rise no higher than his personal estimate of his source. "I am fearfully and wonderfully made . . . and that my soul knoweth right well," sang the Psalmist (Ps. 139). But if the soul does not know this, then it knows something else, and that something else is self-depreciation and a sense of unworthiness.

One psychiatrist has concluded that "the sense of sin is the chief lesion found in mental illness."* A sense of sin is a feeling of unworthiness and self-rejection. The rational mind breaks down when it does not know its source and cannot feel dignified as a result. Because it feels unworthy it expects nothing good. It suspects all men and things as threats and enemies. It makes its home in despair and forboding. As such an emotional pattern develops it becomes compulsive, and even in the midst of dignifying circumstances one is inwardly forced to go home to the old, practiced feeling of unworthiness.

The master thought for such a state is to remember to "call no man your father upon the earth: for one is your Father, which is in heaven" (Matt. 23:9). That is, call nothing on earth the source of your joy or your misery, your hope or your despair, your fear or your faith. Things are what they are. Things are as they are. Let them be as they are. They are not causes; they are results and effects. That which walks and talks and breathes in you is God. It is Cosmic Mind. It is Divine Wisdom. You cannot be separated from it. It goes with you and goes before you.

Your intending mind is the only sovereign agent in your life. There is no other. "Have no other gods before me." The

---

*Quoted by Dr. Allport, ibid.

father of anything is the source of that thing. It is the progenitor of all form and process and experience. There is nothing in this world that can cause you harm until it engages your disposing mind. No person, place, or condition can bless you or hurt you unless and until, by suggestion, it gets your mind's agreement.

This is the glorious liberty of the sons of God, and the sons of God are those who have seen the true Father and know him as their source. The rest, being children of God, unaware of their source, have not yet entered into their sonship and have therefore ascribed the power of creation to things and conditions and people and to all sorts of mental imaginings. The constant or even frequent rehearsal of such thoughts and imaginings trains the emotions to go in the way of sadness and sorrow.

The emotions are the power of our lives. The will or the intention is the steering wheel. Once the emotions have been turned in a certain direction, they are compulsive and ruthless in pursuing that direction. The way to break this trend is to intend the mind in another direction, and especially in the direction of the principle announced above: Call no man (manifestation) on earth your father. Or, stated another way, "It is not what happens to you, but what you think of what happens to you that makes the difference between happiness and misery." Your mind is sovereign, conditions are not. Everything is subject to change. Nothing is forever. Everything is always over. You can be the disposer and the arbiter of this change. As Elijah said to Elisha: "If thou see me [the ideal] when I am taken from thee, it [your request] shall be so unto thee" (2 Kings 2). In other words, if, in the midst of change, your intention and attention are rightly directed, out of the change will come the manifestation of your mind's intent.

Newton was right. When he was asked how he had accomplished so much, he answered, "By intending my mind." By intending the mind you get the emotional car on the tracks to freedom and accomplishment and peace of mind. Andrew Carnegie too discovered this sometime early in his long and productive life, and left the directions for any who might wish to follow. He came to this country as an immigrant boy of thirteen and worked for a dollar a week. Later, in one year alone, he gave away over \$130,000,000. Besides his tremendous business empire and his well-known library and school benefactions, he built a Palace of Peace for the International Court of Arbitration at The Hague and created a \$10,000,000 fund for the Carnegie Endowment for International Peace, as well as building a home for the International Bureau of American Republics in Washington, D.C. In this statement there seems to reside the secret of his achievements: "Tell yourself in your secret reveries, 'I was made to handle affairs.'" The mass mind is always telling us something, some of it good, most of it bad, but the undirected mind has many stops and starts and goes off in many directions. It requires direction. Wherefore, "Every open vessel which hath no covering on it is unclean" (Num. 19). The mind is the vessel referred to. What falls into it conditions it and determines its power, its force, and its movement. The mind, like an open dish, retains whatever comes across its surface. It collects bugs and dust and bacteria and fears and anxieties and impressions of danger and weakness and inferiority. Like the dish, the mind must have its cover "bound upon it." The mind must have a ruling insight, a governing principle by means of which it selects and chooses material that will make up its content. It must have a working principle, a handle by means of which it can manage what comes to it—to separate the sheep from the goats, to exercise its sovereignty and impose peace upon its environment.

In this volume we are dealing almost exclusively with a single principle and I am stating it in a dozen or more different ways, but however expressed, it remains one simple, essential, perennial, imperishable, and demonstrable truth. This single truth is what the Old Bible harps upon as the one Lord. "Hear

O Israel, the Lord is one." There are not two governing powers, there is only one. What seems like a second is only a denial of the one. Any negative thought or emotion is not "another" but simply a limitation of its positive opposite. Negative thoughts and emotions have a power. They are a power. They create. They manifest. But they are only limited degrees of their positive opposites.

Thus fear is a limitation of faith, and anxiety is failure to remember that "they that be for us are greater than they that be against us." The pauper who did not know he was a prince was just as badly off as any of his serfs. It was knowledge of his true status that revealed and established his sovereignty. The same is true of every human being, spiritually speaking. He is born free. He is equipped, commissioned, and ordained to win in the game of life. He has a built-in principle of freedom and sovereignty. But his uncertain knowledge of this principle and experience with it beget his negative experiences. As he climbs the ladder of insight within himself, "then that which is in part shall be done away" because "that which is perfect has come" (1 Cor. 13). The negative is reconciled in the positive, the denial is swallowed up in affirmation and death in life.

There is one recurring, persistent, perennial, and dogging personal problem which, more than any other, steals the force and peace of people and ruins projects and enterprises and careers. It is the habit of feeling hurt because of what others do or do not do and what they say or do not say.

Let me ask you: Do you enjoy a good wrong? Do you find it easy to convince yourself that you have been snubbed, misunderstood, neglected, mistreated, unappreciated, denied, or maligned? No one can condemn another for this reaction, since it is altogether human and common. There are a thousand situations, events, and conditions in everyone's life which can vex and wound and even kill, if one has no defenses against them. "Man's inhumanity to man makes countless thousands mourn." But if you wonder why you are not happier or more successful or healthier, then let these pages make some recommendations for your study and reflection. If you have been on the hot seat too often or too long, perhaps you are seared and roasted enough to be called *done!*

Let the first of these recommendations be couched in the words of one of the most complete men who ever lived, the Emperor of Rome, Marcus Aurelius: "Let your opinion lie still." For we do not suffer from the fact but rather from our opinion of the fact. We suffer from our judgments, our estimates, and our attitudes and not from things and people or events. We expect people to act in a certain way, and when they do not we are disappointed and hurt.

For example, a certain man has been most generous in coming to the aid of others, especially in a financial way. At no little cost to himself, he has loaned and given money to members of his family, his wife's family, and his friends in order to bail them out of their difficulties. He expected gratitude. Does he get it? No! Instead, those he has helped avoid and ignore him. This is often the case. Subsidize a person too much with charity and you make him hate you. For the soul is free and sovereign and wants to stand alone. It hates dependence. But the mind does not always believe in the soul and so accepts dependence, and when the soul in her misery protests at this, the misunderstanding mind projects its dislike upon the one or ones who (it thinks) have put it in this dependent position. Too much sympathy, too much indulgence will usually bring this reaction and for this reason. "Killing with kindness" is more than a phrase. Insecure persons are always putting other insecure persons under financial and emotional obligation because they need the gratitude and the praise of others in order to feel worth in themselves. Such thinking and acting is wandering in the wilderness, going from insult to injury, from offense to wearisome debilitation, harassed and fretted by unseen emotional enemies. The way out is simple: "Let your opinion lie still." Don't judge. Don't expect too much from other people and you will not be disappointed. Expect much from yourself—or better, expect and demand much from Life and its Law, work with the Law and you will not be hurt by what people do or do not do or by what they say and do not say.

"My expectation is from him" (Ps. 62). All things come from one source—the heavenly world, which is the immaterial world, the thought world. It is a world of infinite good, dispensed to each of us according to his conceptions and attitudes. You can have all you want from this source. Why seek a lesser, and then be disappointed and hurt to boot? "Ho, everyone that thirsteth, come ye to the waters, and he that hath no money; come ye, buy, and eat; yea, come, buy wine and milk without money and without price" (Isa. 55) Insofar as our expectation is from this source, we can't be disappointed with people when they fail, and chances are always good that people will do better by us because we do not bind or force them into unreal relationships.

From the Orient comes this old illustration of how people get on the hot seat needlessly and foolishly. You are in a boat on a stream and another boat is approaching at a dangerous angle. The boats are about to collide. Anger rises in you and you are about to explode in words of outrage at whoever is steering the other boat. Presently you discover that the boat is empty. Your wrath subsides; you are not angry at the boat. But now a second glance shows you that there is a man in the boat and your blood begins to boil again. The story illustrates how conditioned we are by the assumption that people ought to act in certain prescribed ways; when they do not we are offended or outraged or humiliated or provoked or maddened, or simply annoyed. In any case we are hurt, and all without reason. For at such times we have forgotten our guiding principle that nothing can happen to us that is not a part of our own consciousness. As Marjorie Wilson wrote in one of her fine books: You are asleep in your bed and some mean person comes to your bedside and excoriates you in words of scorn and abuse. When will it hurt you? Only when you waken and hear the words and make them a part of your consciousness.*

Take a look at the same truth as Coué illustrated it. You are on an English Channel steamer. The sea is very rough and a number of people are ill. You notice a young lady standing near the rail. You realize that she is almost at the limit of her control, and you say to her: "Miss Smith, you look a little pale. Are you ill?" That is all it takes to send Miss Smith bending and retching over the rail. Your suggestion has touched off her own expectation and fear. If the possibility of sickness had not been dominant in her consciousness, your suggestion would have had no effect. To prove this, go up to an old sailor who has been sailing the seas all his life and say the same thing to him. "Jack, you look a little peaked. Are you feeling sick?" He will scorn your suggestion, as he scorns the rough weather. In fact your words will only serve to trigger off the conviction of his superiority to the weather which he has established by long experience. If what is within you is strong and right, even a negative suggestion will do no harm but rather make you stronger and turn things to your account.

"Judge not," the Book of Wisdom advises about people and events and situations and all the changing scene. Don't look at any of these with expectation of harm or blessing, for they are not causes but simply avenues. In your moment of judgment of something or someone as source of displeasure or harm, it is not only the something or someone that is judged, but you yourself. For your judgment is a measure of your own mood. Your judgment is your opinion, and your opinion is your life at the moment. Let your opinion lie still and you do not suffer.

There is an old Chinese view of this royal indifference to the color and cast of events. A young man captured a wild horse, a fine animal. He brought him home to his father, and neighbors and friends all gathered to rejoice with them and ex-

* *Your Personality and God* (Philadelphia: J.B. Lippincott Co., 1938), pp. 80–81.

claimed, "What good luck!" But the father of the youth said, "What's good, what's bad?"

The youth mounted the horse to break him to the saddle, and the animal threw him and broke his leg. Now the friends and neighbors gathered again to sympathize and commiserate. "Ah, what bad luck!" Again the father shrugged his shoulders and said, "What's good, what's bad?"

Next day, officers of the army came to the house recruiting young men for service, and they passed over the youth with the broken leg. Once more the neighbors and friends came to rejoice: "Oh, what good luck!" And the old man shrugged again and said, "What's good, what's bad?"

Another way by which people get onto the hot seat and sizzle there is the tendency to be in constant distress and turmoil over the fact that things are as they are and not as they ought to be. Even old Omar felt the need to "dash this sorry world to bits, and then/Remold it closer to the heart's desire." Why do big fish eat little fish? Why is nature "red in tooth and claw?" Why should there be cataclysms and earthquakes and tornadoes and war and disease? Why does God allow these things? Why does he allow innocent little children to suffer, and why should the wicked prosper like the green bay tree?" In short, what is the origin of evil, and how do we handle it —a difficulty every system of thought has had to meet. We shall deal with the question at more length in a later chapter; here it will be helpful merely to follow the advice of the Emperor when he says, "Does your cucumber taste bitter?— let it alone. Are there brambles in your way?—avoid them then. Thus far you are well. But, then, do not ask 'What does the world with such things as this?' for a natural philosopher would laugh at you."* "Be willing to have it so" is a modern counsel for this kind of mental distress.

I have a friend of eighty-seven summers who has achieved much and kept his equanimity and geniality throughout. He

---

*Marcus Aurelius, *Meditations,* Jeremy Collier, trans. (London: Walter Scott, Ltd.), Bk. VIII, par. 50.

said to me once, "I never let the weather interfere with what I want to do." Things and happenings in nature can be called good and evil only from the relative point of view of the individual, for all proceeds from one Cosmic Designer. To suggest that the design is a mixture of good and evil components is to imply that the Designer did not know his business, also that the creation is not a cosmos or order but a contradiction and conflict. And the mind that thinks this way becomes a malcontent of the first order. It rails against heaven but succeeds only in disturbing its own house.

Good and evil are matters of opinion and therefore within the power of the person. He can choose. He is the arbiter of his own destiny and not the blind pawn of an unheeding fate. What do you think of a happening or a situation? Does it threaten you? Resort to your rule of thumb: "There is nothing good or bad but thinking makes it so." Continue reflecting on this rule of thumb and understand that it is what you think of this situation that governs you and not the situation itself. Causation is always in mind and not in things. The idea of good and evil as wholly a matter of opinion and therefore entirely within our personal power forestalls the tendency to irritability and complaint. Stay with the rule and you have no urge to remonstrate with heaven or quarrel with any stick or stone. As the old saying has it, "Keep to the score and thou hast not to fear."

Is there anything now to be hot about? Do you know now how to keep your cool? This is not to suggest that you will never be hot again and will always be calm and cool as a Buddha. For we have all been conditioned to become hot and exercised over many things, and now the process of reconditioning must begin. Think of the many expressions that indicate how people have given away their power to things and conditions and allowed their emotions to run riot. "I was devastated" or "overwhelmed." "I was struck dumb!" or "I was burned up!" or "How shocking, how diabolical!" Each of these expressions is an example of overreaction, of suffering from a judgment and letting an opinion make more of a situation than it otherwise warrants. And now you have a handle by which to deal with every such situation. Whenever your pot starts bubbling and hot waters of emotion tend to overflow, bring out your rule of thumb and remember: opinion governs —facts and things and situations are neutral. Have no opinion about the goodness or badness of a situation, and it will not move or affect you. Withhold your judgment and you do not suffer. Don't make more of a thing than your senses report. If your first reaction was "Oh how terrible!" react again and let your opinion lie still, and quickly your peace will return to you. Now not the situation but *you* govern and control. Is someone you love sick? That does not say he is going to be worse off or that he is going to die; that is only your opinion, drawn from many past impressions and from the experience of the mass mind. Be bold to withhold the opinion and cease to judge the situation. As your peace returns it will be communicated in waves of strength to the sick one. You do not have to help him or try to heal him. You only have to know the truth about the situation, cancel your fear, and come to peace. Then Truth heals him.

Has someone maligned and gossiped about you and said unfair and untrue things? As the heat rises in you, apply the cooling effect of the principle: someone has said bad things about you, but that you are bad because he said so does not follow. That is his opinion, and he suffers from it. Help him to recover from the error of that opinion if you can. If you can't, leave him to heaven, restore your own good opinion of yourself, and walk on. If his words have hit home and you feel guilty, forgive yourself by remembering that all mortals are guilty of coming short of the full stature of a perfect human being. If you had thought differently, you would have done differently. Now you are thinking differently, so you will do differently. Being a different person in consciousness now, you cannot be condemned for the acts of the person you were.

You are being sued for a large sum of money. It is more

money than you own or than you can borrow. Do not conclude that you are faced with financial ruin, for this is not reported in the news of the suit. Keep your thought of the situation clean, don't import factors that are not there, treat to dissipate your fear of false imaginings of "what may happen," and thus keep your inner parts clothed in poise and courage. Then these inner parts, being indeed the divine majesty within you, will send their atmosphere ahead of you and defend you better than a battery of lawyers, and even perhaps adjudicate the case in your favor before the lawyers ever speak. "God in the midst of you is mighty."

Here then is your handle for getting off the hot seat. A handle is for handling. Use it, and rejoice that all the devils of this world are subject unto you.

How to Control Your Mind

If you have accepted the rule that it is not what is happening *to* you but rather what is happening *in* you that determines whether you succeed or fail, you already have in your hands a handle by means of which you can control the fractious mind. All that we are seeing in these pages, from beginning to end, is a statement and a restatement of this single principle in as many ways as possible. It is your opinion that matters. Your opinion is your governing principle. Withhold your opinion on any matter and that matter immediately becomes neutral in your world. Only when something "gets to you" can it work in you and through you. It has no life of its own. It borrows life from you or from your mind.

Swirling around your mind at this moment are all sorts of intimations, suggestions, and intrusive impressions trying to take up an abode in your consciousness. Allow them residence and they will soon become star boarders, and as with the fabled Arab and his camel, you will be pushed out of your own home. Your mind will become the child of propaganda or the mere manipulated instrument of impressions and suggestions from the world around you. And not only from the perceptible world around you, but also from the psychic sea in which we all live. In this psychic sea, the undisciplined and unorganized thoughts and emotions of all the world are moving like vast currents in the physical ocean, and they can and often do overwhelm the personal mind with tidal waves of fear and despair and common nervousness.

The mind that does not know itself and its intrinsic power is constantly amenable to suggestion from a thousand sources, most of them negative and debilitating. But when the mind knows itself as the sole arbiter of its experience, it is no longer amenable to false fears because it is full of its own confidence. A vessel that is full can receive no more. In this regard, the Master Mind speaks in self-description: "The prince of this world cometh and hath nothing in me" (John 14). When all the content of the mind is organized around this central principle, it is no longer amenable to fear. It knows the Truth and the Truth has set it free. For the mind is amenable only to thoughts which are like its own content. No others can enter. This is well-documented and proven but it is sufficient for the present only to recall the case of the young woman and the old sailor on the channel boat.

In my early practice I had a dramatic example of how "nerves" are learned and may be unlearned. A friend of mine sent a friend of his to me for instruction in these matters. He was a nervous man who was holding two jobs, as a professor and as an editor. He was so nervous that the only way he could work was to pull out the middle drawer of his desk every hour or so and take a barbiturate. He had a sad, unhappy look, and for good reason. While a young professor at a midwestern school he had bought a new car and taken his fiancee out for a drive. A train demolished the car, killed his fiancee, and sent him to the hospital for agonizing weeks. He had had other car-train collisions, and these and certain other negative experiences had set up in his mind a pattern of vulnerability to misfortune. He said: "I am the kind of man who, if he is standing on the railroad siding, a train will jump the track and hit me." We spent many weeks examining the handle together and depositing in his mind a content of insights which displaced the old content of nervous impressions. We have seen earlier in these pages that the mind is a hopper, a collector of opinions, and that the chief opinion is the ruler and maker of experience. At the end of our sessions, I reminded him how he had first described himself to me: as a person prone to accident and trouble, and he smiled in relaxed satisfaction and announced, "Thank God, I'm not that kind of a man any more."

The unorganized mind will always be restless until its content is reordered. P. P. Quimby observed that every child's mind is like a blank tablet upon which everyone who comes along makes a scribble. Many of these scribblings have a fear content and become self-acting agents of nervousness. Years later, some sight or sound or circumstance can trigger off a sleeping impression and arouse feelings of fear and anxiety or rage and resentment. Because the deep content of the mind is subconscious, and because the subconscious is the seat of the emotions, this first manifestation of the mind content is emotional or what is called "nerves." But it is not the nerves that are at fault. Nerves are only the carriers of emotion, and emotion is thought or mind on the move.

The mind is like the ocean, ceaselessly moving. Therefore, when we speak of controlling it we do not mean control in an absolute sense but in a regulatory sense. So much of the mind is always acting on its own account. You cannot turn it off or stop it altogether. Many times we wish we could. Oh, to be delivered from the ceaseless flow of thoughts and images that sometimes oppress the human mind! Even in sleep there is no cessation of this flow of images through the mind; it continues at a subsconscious level in dreams.

All elemental forces are greater than we, but we can modify them and regulate them and manage their power in relation to ourselves. The sun and wind, water, fire, gas, electricity, and all natural forces have a universal quality and do not bend to the personal and individual will of man except as he first obeys the general laws of their nature. Mind is the universal force individualized in humans for individual experience, and our control of it comes through first understanding it and its law. With mind, as with all other universal forces, the old rule holds true, "Nature obeys us in proportion as we first obey nature."

Many centuries ago, Oriental thinkers recognized that the mind is a constant mover and that it is next to impossible to stop it altogether. But one can learn to manage it by skillful use of the handle of control. They compared the mind to a jumping monkey.* To intensify the image, they added that the monkey was maddened; then someone got him drunk; and finally, a scorpion bit him.

Hardly a better picture could be drawn of the average nervous mind. It is always restless because of its inner conditioning and its constant amenability to the stimuli of its environment. It flits hither and yon all the time in response to sights and sounds and smells and tastes, and is always eager for more information, even if it hurts. Notice how the average mind is eager to listen to gossip, to look at the gruesome and grotesque, to taste the exotic. A noise in the room will cause most heads to turn to look at the cause of it—so little is the attention under the direction of the will, but rather at the mercy of events.

These and other examples suggest to us how the jumping-monkey nature of our mind leads us about, continually giving attention to this, that, and the other, for we are not in control, but the automonous motion of the mind controls us. As a Shakespearean scholar recently observed about the modern novel: "It is full of a lot of four-letter words which keep the average reader sniffing through the pages like a dog in a garbage can on the scent of a rotten bone." That is the way the mind works. It is a rover. It is a wanderer.

*See Swami Vivekananda's *What Religion Is* (New York: Julian Press, 1963), pp. 112–13.

The first step in getting control of the jumping monkey is to *let it jump.* Practice watching it jump. Get amused with its jumping—stand apart and look at the mind and watch it. Be objective with it, all the while trying to sense who it is that is observing. This is the first step in controlling the mind, for what you can observe is not you. Very soon you will realize that you are not the mind, but stand behind it and use it as an instrument. As soon as you realize this you will have a bit of leverage over it. You will get a sense of yourself as separate from what is happening to you and in you. The real you which stands behind the mind is never worried, never concerned, never exhausted. The agitation is entirely in the senses.

An old Buddhist illustration points this up. A young man went to the sage for instruction and said, "Master, I have a terrible temper. Can you cure me of it?" The Master said, "Show this temper to me." The young man answered, "Well, I cannot show it to you just now. It comes and goes." Whereupon the sage said, "Then it is no part of you." Learn to deal with all the fractious movements of the mind in just this way. Follow the rule, "It is not what is happening to me but rather what I think of what is happening to me that determines my way. Let the monkey jump until he gets tired, for tired he will get as I continue to observe him and thus assert the difference between his errant movements and my sovereign self."

One cannot stop the mind, but one can control it by this exercise in observation, and then later by reflection and by applying the law of substitution. There is an old Tamil tale which shows how the mind can be distracted for evil but also gives us some fine insights into control of it. A wandering fakir came to a certain village and announced that he had discovered a wonderful secret: he knew how to make gold. All that was needed was to put certain ingredients in a pot and stir them well until the gold appeared. But first, fees had to be paid to the fakir by everyone in the village. Then the head man of the village would do the stirring of the pot—for the fakir made no gold himself; he only told others how to do it. When all these preliminaries were finished and the head man was ready to stir the pot, the fakir announced that one condition still was lacking. "While you are stirring, you must on no account allow yourself to think of a red-faced monkey." While the villagers were watching their head man stir the pot, the fakir left with his bag of fees.

The story illustrates the formidable power of suggestion. How can that head man not think of a red-faced monkey? Here is a power that moves and dominates the world more than any other single force. The world moves largely by suggestion, and those who can implant suggestion govern those who receive it. Those who are suggested to do not realize that they give their power away through this law. The head man cannot fail to think of a red-faced monkey. And why? Because he is greedy, It is just at this point that he is suggestible. If he were not greedy he would not have fallen for the old shell game in another form.

How often we read in the newspapers of people being mulcted of their life's savings by some con man. How did it happen? How could they have been so foolish? In one instance a woman was told to put all her savings in a brown paper bag and bring it to a certain address at a certain time, and she would double her money. Of course she lost it. How could she have been so foolish? She was greedy. She expected something for nothing. And so the suggestion that she could get something for nothing triggered off her own belief and motivation. That is how suggestion works—always in terms of what is dominant in a person's consciousness.

Of American boys who were taken prisoner in Korea and brainwashed by the enemy, the only ones to survive in any number were those who had some strong religious conviction. It did not make any difference what the religion was so long as the person had a strong belief in it. There is no technique of suggestion more formidable than that employed by the Communist brainwashers. Yet here is evidence that their diabolical methods met up with something stronger. You cannot suggest fear and make it stick with a man who has a minimal content of fear inside.

The Master Teacher taught men to seek first the kingdom of heaven and its righteousness, and all these things for which we strain—and in straining cause so much misery and pain, jealousy and ambition and hurt feelings and animosity and fear —all these things would be added to us if we sought the kingdom of heaven first. Unfortunately, the kingdom of heaven concept has not yet received its new hearing and understanding in this world. To many people it is something beyond the skies or some sort of utopia or millennium—as may be seen by the anecdote of The Texas businessman who tried to phone a man in New York, only to be told by the secretary that he was in the United Kingdom. "My God!" exclaimed the startled Texan. "Is it too late for flowers?"

But the kingdom of heaven concept should not be projected to another time and place. The kingdom of heaven is the government of consciousness. It is the authoritative control of the mind and its moods. We have seen how the mind can be controlled by suggestion or through the sundry impressions of the wandering senses. But in spiritual science understanding takes control of all these mental motions and sits like a king on his throne in the midst of them. Heaven means the immaterial realm, and the only immaterial realm we know is consciousness or mind or thought. It is here that sovereignty must be exercised. If this is done, all other things go well. Seek first the kingdom of heaven and its righteousness—or right action—and all the things you strive and strain for will come as a result.

If we take control of this kingdom, our talents prosper and our ambitions are realized in divine order, and we become more relaxed individuals. Our efforts are no longer based upon the stratagems of the world but rather upon knowing the spiritual law. There is then no straining for the pelf of this world any more, and we are therefore not subject to blackmail or fear, or to jealousy or greed or any of the corroding emotions. It is only where we are weak in these matters that the world can hurt us. Greed is a weakness, and its presence in any one of us makes him vulnerable to the suggestions and tricks of dishonest people, whereby they may get hold of what little he has. Wherever there is greed or overweening ambition, or thought of the personal self apart and separate from a divine being, there is weakness and a consequent susceptibility to weakening suggestion.

Shakespeare's *Timon of Athens* is a good illustration. The Athenian lord is a well-placed noble, honored by all. He loves to do good and to give money and art and precious things to others. This is his weakness, for he does these things so that men may praise him, and lives only for praise. At this point he can be hurt. He gives great banquets and invites the "friends of his heart." He does not realize that they are friends of his purse, and that any chronic receiver secretly disdains his benefactor because his constant taking makes him feel like a beggar. We ought never give to another so much that we make him feel dependent and beggarly. Timon finally runs out of cash, and all his friends decamp. Now Timon becomes a hater and despiser of men: "I am misanthropos and hate mankind."

If your love is so fatuous as to be based upon the flattery of others, then you are in danger. Your love of the false is actually disregard of the true and will be so demonstrated.

The next great step in controlling the mind is to realize that we have no immediate control of our minds. Ideas do. Ideas control the mind, and we can control ideas by the simple act of choice in entertaining them. Any idea that lodges in the mind, first consciously and then subconsciously, will grow and exert an influence and finally become self-active and compulsive. Freud dramatized the negative aspect of this rule or law. Modern metaphysical instruction is always endeavoring to emphasize the same law in its positive aspect: a good idea exalted in the mind will become a governor in the mind and a ruler of the individual's actions, and will compel him for good just as a bad idea exalted in the mind will compel him for evil.

How ideas are compulsive may readily be seen in the phenomena of hypnotism. Hypnosis is a state of mind in which the conscious or reasoning mind relaxes or goes to sleep and ceases to function. To reason means to deal with two or more alternatives. The subconscious mind, on the other hand, is a one-track mind. It can deal with only one idea at a time. When the conscious mind is in abeyance, the subconscious part of the mind is said to be susceptible to suggestion. When an idea gets lodged in the subconscious mind, it is compulsive and king-like. That is why people say in regard to a negative compulsion, "I couldn't help myself. I was compelled" to do or to say a thing.

Many years ago I knew a salesman who traveled a poor territory. He was a hard worker, but he never was able to make more than about five thousand a year. His superiors watched his manly struggles and decided to reward him with a rich territory which was good for at least thirty thousand. But in this rich territory, too, he made only five thousand. For one thing, he fell sick for three months out of the year. His consciousness arranged it that way. In his deep thought about himself, he was a five-thousand-a-year man. He was compelled by an absolute within him, and regardless of conditions, his experience would not change until he had deposed this faulty ruler and exalted a better one.

We must first bind the strong man before we can spoil his goods. There is a strong man in the subconscious of each and everyone of us. It is the person's ruling idea about himself and his life experience. So often it is a negative concept of failure, poor health, or some other limitation. It sits like the dragon in the Nordic myths hoarding a pile of gold, in this case the unrealized capacities and talents and strengths of the person. Not until a Siegfried comes along and slays the dragon will the gold be available.

So take Carnegie's wonderful axiom and tell yourself in your secret reveries, "I was made to rule." Or take a statement from Thoreau and work with either of them, or both. Thoreau said, "Men are born to succeed, not to fail." Reflect on this until you accept it. Eat its substance and drink its blood or the inspiring influence that flows from it, and it will exalt itself in you, rule you, and compel you to succeed rather than to fail. The more you think about an idea like this, the more control you will get over the ambitious part of your mind, over that mind which wants personal honors, personal flattery, personal wealth, and all sorts of personal aggrandizements. We are always weak to the extent that we depend upon these. We are strong when we get behind them and know who we are as spiritual beings with dominion and power—not power over people, but power over our own thoughts. Then, when bad news arrives or distressing circumstances come, the mind tends to remain poised and undisturbed. It retains its force. It may cry, it may weep, it may be set back by the news, but it will soon recover and go on to victory.

Thoreau's statement may be only a pretty saying to you now, only a bit of philosophy. But reflect frequently upon it and it will release its potencies in you. That is what is meant by "eating its body and drinking its blood." The old theology pondered much upon this theme, but not always with practical enlightment. The wafer and the wine are symbols, but they remain just that until the meaning leaves the symbol and becomes living reality. Psychologically speaking, the meaning is this: Take any true idea (Truth is a synonym for Christ) and eat it—that is, reflect upon it, appropriate it in your thought; savor it until it releases its fullness to your insight. That is "eating its body and drinking its blood." All true ideas are food for the mind and blood or vitality for the whole being. Do you not feel better when you hear this, "Men are born to succeed and not to fail?" That feeling is the blood and the substance being released to you. That is the blood of the New Testament, or the new dispensation in your life.

You were born to succeed because you come of a divine source. That brings us to the last step in learning control of the mind. If you believe that in your deep origin you are divine, keep telling yourself so. That is the way constructive suggestion works. The subconscious will not believe you if you say it once. It wants to hear you say it again and again, for it will act only upon what you unequivocally believe. Say it when you are prayerful and reflective, say it when you are active and deliberative, and say it when you are challenged and strained. As Isaiah announces, "When the enemy shall come in like a flood, the spirit of the Lord shall lift up a standard against him." When the enemy of fear or anxiety assails you, raise this truth in consciousness. Up with the flag! Let fear or worry or agitation serve only to remind you to think this truth. When distress comes, you don't have to deny the condition. Simply look at it and say, Thank you for reminding me to know the truth—because I come from a divine source I am fated to succeed. I was born free, inheriting the nature of my divine source. That which is happening in me now is more important than what is happening *to* me. In spite of how I feel, what I am now knowing is ruling and governing and prospering me.

chapter 4

Thinking the Unthinkable

As we have seen, suggestion is a very real force in our lives—always has been and always will be. It operates at the level where our own convictions are weakest or nonexistent. Our only protection is to have healthy, strong convictions ourselves, especially convictions based upon the great Mind Principle and the truth that opinion governs. The creative handling of trouble is to *think the unthinkable.* The way in which we think about it is to put it in its place, to understand it for what it is, and to think and establish our own position in regard to it. Then we are free.

When President Kennedy was assassinated there was a great deal of comment upon the fact that there is a baleful pattern in the elections and deaths of Presidents every twenty years, beginning with 1840. Every President elected at these twenty-year intervals since 1840 has either died or been assassinated while in office. The pattern began with the election of Harrison in 1840. He died in office. Then came Lincoln in 1860 and Garfield in 1880 and McKinley in 1900, all of whom were assassinated. Next came Harding and Roosevelt in 1920 and 1940 respectively and finally Kennedy in 1960.

President Kennedy is reported to have been reminded of

this pattern after his election and was asked what he thought about it. He is said to have replied laughingly, "Well, I'll break that rule." Then later the question was asked, "Why didn't he do it?" My answer was at the time, and is today: perhaps he did not take it seriously—perhaps he did not really believe it. But every threat of trouble, even if it is a superstition, is a real thing in the mind and must be taken seriously. People usually do not take these things seriously, or if they do they don't know what to do about them.

I am saying in this chapter that we must take these things seriously and give some thought to the unthinkable before it happens, in order to prevent the likelihood of its happening. We may consider it superstitious and unworthy of an enlightened mind to believe in these things, but what we forget is that we all live in a psychic sea of other men's thoughts and beliefs. Here is a pattern which has been known and believed by millions and even if a great part of their thinking is superstitious, their combined thought is a vital thing and something to be reckoned with. The psychic sea of other men's thoughts —their beliefs and superstitions, their fears and anxieties as well as their hopes and desires, their confidence and peace and harmony—swirls all about us. It is the mental atmosphere in which we all live, and its strongest elements can and do invade our personal minds wherever we are weakest in our spiritual convictions. Whenever the mind of mankind as a whole, or in some very large segment, tends to believe very strongly in some danger, even if its reasons are superstitious we cannot afford to ignore this "racial" belief (in the sense of the human race) and suppose that we are unaffected by it, if we have done no reflecting upon it. Whenever the general thought concerned presents itself, we have to do our own individual mental work in and upon ourselves and so establish our position in regard to it. This mental work has to be done repeatedly. We have to be our own enlightened hypnotist, or else the "racial" mind will hypnotize us according to its beliefs.

It is not pleasant to contemplate the possibility of trouble or harm and therefore many people do not. I say you must contemplate it, not to the point of morbidly falling under its spell, but to the point of declaring and knowing your spiritual transcendency. "Come ye out from among them," and come frequently and repeatedly.

That is what I mean by thinking the unthinkable—not thinking it to the point of fear, but thinking it to the point of establishing freedom and independence from it. A prophecy is not a fact. It is only a prophecy, and it has been pointed out (1 Cor. 13) that under certain conditions of spiritual insight, prophecies fail. A prophecy is not actual, it is only prospective. It can become actual in us if we afford it room or acceptance. You can deny its acceptance by looking at it, thinking about it in accordance with spiritual truth, and establishing your position of transcendency concerning it.

We fall into trouble in two ways: either by consciously thinking limiting thoughts or by allowing thoughts of limitation to be thought in us on the involuntary level. Suggestion of evil does not and cannot work in the mind that is full of Truth. We cannot disregard the evil around us. We cannot say that the devil does not exist, that he is a superstition, that evil is only misplaced good and that we are children of God, and then do nothing more. We must face the unthinkable, think out our position in relation to it, and so decide.

What is the most fearsome thing you can think of? Death? Paul says that is the last enemy to be overcome. Have you thought about death? That may seem quite negative to some, to call death to mind. It is unwise, however, to keep pushing it away, for it will not go away until you face it, think about it, and establish your position of freedom about it. It is said that the coward dies a thousand deaths, the brave man but one. The coward has never thought out his position about death and so dies every time the threat arises. The brave man knows that man can die but once and therefore does not ascribe to every fearful event the gravity of the final one.

How to think the unthinkable and rise about it is well

illustrated in the experience of Colonel Lindbergh, flying his little sprucewood plane across the Atlantic. As he left the last stretches of land in Nova Scotia and Newfoundland, he kept looking down on the forests and lakes and valleys and thinking that if an emergency arose he would land in that little clearing beside the river, or he would clear that clump of trees and land in that lake. Superficial minds would say that he was thinking of trouble, and indeed he was, but transcendently. He was thinking the unthinkable and defeating it mentally before it ever arose. He was seeking and finding his strong position in regard to every possible contingency and so was overcoming the threat of it, eliminating it from his mind as a source of worry and concern. Then it was finished business and he could give his attention to the important business of navigation.

Margaret Bourke - White, the famous journalist-photographer, was trained by her mother to face trouble, look at it, and establish a transcendent relationship to it. As a child, she often woke in the night and would think there were burglars downstairs; whereupon her oldest sister, Ruth, would take her by the hand and say, "Come, let's take a look." They would go from room to room looking for the presumed burglar until finally, when little Margaret came to the last room, she felt so strong that had there been an actual intruder there she could have faced him unafraid. By this ritual the two girls had lifted themselves above the unthinkable.

We all have a built-in power to transcend trouble. Power is available to us, as available as electricity and air and uranium in the ground, as gasoline in crude oil, as fertility in the earth. We have to lay hold upon it—that is our work. Providence has provided. Our work is to receive and to use. "Before they call, I will answer and while they are yet speaking I will hear" (Isa. 65). That was a good prayer of the old gentleman who said, "O Lord, help me to understand that you are not going to let anything happen to me that you and I together cannot handle."

Right thinking or mental treatment or prayer ought not to

be an effort to make something happen, but rather an effort to know and accept the fact that all we can ever want has already happened. How can Life answer before we have asked, unless it has already anticipated every human need and prepared it in the mind-stuff of the universe, whence it may be appropriated by any individual mind? Edison confided that his whole work consisted of "plucking surprises out of the unknown." Consider how your desire for something is an indication that that something is a reality—not a substantial reality, to be sure, but nevertheless a reality in mind, or you could not think of it. The mind cannot think of nothing. You cannot desire nothing. The mind has apprehended the near-presence of something or it would not desire it.

Think of our allusion to the little baby in his crib. Your are playing with him. He notices your shiny wrist watch and his little hand reaches for it. If he had not seen it, he would not have desired it. To the child, anything he sees and wants is his, and he will reach mind and hand to take it. His desire is authorization for possession. And the child is right. But there is a *way* in which he is right. His parents and teachers and society are right, too, in teaching him that he cannot have what belongs to another.

Yet in a certain sense they are wrong. Shouting "don'ts" and "shalt nots" at him may offend that basic wisdom which whispers deep within and announces that anything he sees belongs to him by right of consciousness. He may grow up within the strictures of the law that prohibits theft and offense to others, but his desire remains. It is the primal thrust. Desire is the beginning of all action and effort. "It was the desire to fly that gave the gods their wings." E-motion is "motion from" within to an objective without. In the healthy mind this emotional flow is unrestrained ever surging forward, surmounting all annoyances, cascading over problems and, in the poet's imagery, "hurrying amain to reach the plain" of fulfillment and achievement. In the sick mind, the emotional flow is contrary, circular, flowing back, and that is why the sick mind spits and spews and belches inhumanities.

The great psychological tensions of life are built up when this primal thrust of desire is impeded. Then the free flow of emotional life is dammed up and takes on the character of extremes. Love turns to hate, and envy and malevolence are born. Examine the life of the average criminal and you will find this inner turmoil with a projection of its cause onto society, because the true cause is unknown to him. We always project onto others, says Dr. Jung, what is unconscious in ourselves; but the cause of our individual hurt is never in others but in our own ignorance of the great Mind Principle. Desire is like an arrow. Its home is in that which is desired. When it is home, that is union. Love is union. "Yea, the sparrow hath found an house and the swallow a nest for herself, where she may lay her young, even thine altars, O Lord of hosts, my King and my God" (Ps. 84:3). Where there is no union, there is division, separation, lowliness, and estrangement. The soul alone is victim of a thousand furies. Divested of its garments, it is naked in the storm. The elements torture it and every sound is a threat. Like an animal at bay, it lashes out at anything within reach. Not having found love, it has found hate. Union is love and love is union. Let someone show the soul its inborn, imperishable uprightness and it will move again in love and be united with its beloved.

The child's impulse is correct. Whatever it beholds and wants belongs to it, but only by right of consciousness. No need to possess that which belongs to another. The physical thing the child sees is an idea, an idea made manifest. It is an external image of an inner reality—a mental image. In maturity, the child may learn to appropriate the image by mental means alone—that image or prototype by which the Infinite has already answered every heart's desire. When the mind is spiritually mature, it knows that to possess the internal image is to possess all. The external image will inevitably appear. Somewhere in this is the true foundation and rationale of all morality.

Between desire and the desire fulfilled stands the adversary.
The adversary is the belief that God has a second, that spirit
is not sole and only creator, that the forms of the spirit are
greater than that which made them. The adversary is any
opinion or belief or notion that people or conditions are not
subservient to attitudes.

Dr. Viktor Frankl, who spent three years in Auschwitz, tells
how "the medical men among us learned first of all that the
textbooks tell lies."* Having been stripped and shaved and
showered the first night, the prisoners were made to stand
naked and wet in the chill, open, autumn air for a protracted
period. They were amazed to discover that they did not catch
cold. All the textbooks said that men in this condition would
catch cold and contract pneumonia and perhaps die. The medical men among them were angry when they discovered that
the textbooks did not know what they were talking about.

These men were in another dimension of mind. Hope was
largely gone; the statistical chances of survival were one in
twenty. Their experience ought to help anyone to loosen the
hold of that slavish opinion that believes our bodies are subject
to the weather and its vagaries. I would warn the reader not
to take this statement too lightly. Do not deliberately go and
test it and get wet just to see if it works. That would be
tempting the Lord. Don't do anything for which you have not
the consciousness. Only the prepared and conditioned consciousness can insure success in any endeavor. Mere hopes and
wishes and idealistic fancies will only end in disaster. But let
Dr. Frankl's experience extend the area of your consciousness
to include the fact that the spirit is always transcendent of its
matter. Nearly all people, if you ask them, would credit this
statement. But many of them would credit it as a philosophy
and not as an experience. Just as the doctors in Auschwitz
might have agreed that the spirit is transcendent, but nevertheless, if you are wet and stand naked in the cold air you will

* *The Search for Meaning* (Beacon, Rev. Ed., 1963).

catch cold. When they had the actual experience of transcending their environment, their belief was no longer a mere philosophical assent but a conscious and memorable experience which could not be doubted.

Keep extending your area of consciousness to include every miracle you have ever heard of or read about. There is a dimension of mind where even poisons do not kill. Again, I would not favor or countenance those religious practices by which people whip themselves into a fervor and then allow rattlesnakes to bite them, in order to prove their faith. This kind of practice can often lead to grief. But if, in the normal performance of your duty, you should be bitten by a snake or otherwise exposed to poison, know that there is deliverance through the transcendence of the spirit.

Better still, know it now and reflect upon it until you condition your consciousness to accept deliverance now from any threatening event that might befall you. Go over in your mind the tragedies and losses that have befallen men or might befall them and think what you would do in similar circumstances and how you would want to act. Buttress your thought with frequent reference to the great Mind Principle and know that, to you as to all men, the promise has been given of deliverance and freedom and health and happiness. Meet the adversary frequently in your thought and take his measure—the adversary of fear and doubt and misgivings and despair and depression. I repeat, this is not negative thinking but truly constructive thinking. Overcome your fear now and you will not need to pray for courage when the clouds gather, for where there is no fear, courage is unnecessary. This is the path of the wise and the just and the accomplished in all walks of life.

War offers many examples of this saving dimension of mind. I have a dear friend whose son was in the Canadian Army in Holland during World War II. During those grim days, the mother was in almost constant prayer, surrounding her son with the protecting presence. A shell wrecked the jeep in which he was riding, and all the occupants were presumed dead. A farmer, passing the scene, noticed that the little finger on the son's body seemed to move. Help was summoned, and the man lives today. Some will say that that experience was just a lucky break, or fate. But I say that fate is made and remade every day by prayer.

In that same war, the late Brigadier General Theodore Roosevelt landed at Omaha Beach, which was already littered with dead. Enemy guns from up on the cliffs were sending a murderous fire directly onto the beach, and a few survivors were huddled whimpering under the cliffs. Roosevelt surveyed the situation quickly and carrying nothing but his officer's stick walked up and down the beach, rallying those boys and reassuring them: "You see, they can't hit me, and they can't hit you either." He rallied them, and they took the cliffs and put out the guns and went on across Normandy.

The ageless wisdom does not lie, and it does not speak in fairy tales and fantasies when it says that you can take up serpents, and if you drink any deadly thing it shall not hurt you. There is a dimension of mind where this holds true. If you are doing your proper work with the proper motivation, if you have a cause and a purpose and it glorifies you enough to lift you above the petty vexations and worries of your environment, you may not have time to think about it but you can count on something above and beyond your own efforts and skills. There is a place in mind or consciousness which is security from all kinds of earthly trouble. Lao Tze says that when the sage goes forth, he carries no sword and no spear and is not afraid of javelin or the tooth of rhinoceros, because there is in him no place where these can enter.

"Be not overcome of evil, but overcome evil with good" (Rom. 12). How do we do this? Certainly not by fighting evil directly and frontally. This only reinfects the fighter and magnifies the evil. The lion was challenged by a skunk, and the lion refused the encounter with dignity, saying, "I could easily dispatch you with one sweep of my paw, but that would be no

honor to me, for everywhere I went people would know that
I had been fighting with you." Trying to overcome an external
irritant without first overcoming it inwardly is an assumption
that the irritant has a primary existence in and of itself (rather
than being the shadow cast by an opaqueness in the one ir-
ritated), and every assumption of the mind gives some substance of reality to the thing assumed and projects it as an
experience. Thus the more one fights the irritant, the more
vitality one gives it. Countless thousands go around and
around in this vicious circle every day. Evil is never in what
is happening to us, but rather in what we think about what is
happening to us. That is the evil that must be overcome.

Some have supposed that Paul's admonition means that
goodness is permissiveness and gentleness in the face of injury. They have often gone so far as to suggest that being kind
and gentle and meek and generous with ugly people will
overcome their meanness. Many a woman has married a man,
believing that her generous outpouring of love alone will
reform his nature. And many in religion and philosophy have
felt and thought that by merely being kind to an oppressor one
can tame him. But one cannot always overcome strength with
weakness, and mere kindness without knowledge of the mental law is weakness. It is like the story of the little boy at school.
He was continually being bullied by an older boy named Billy.
Each evening he would come home with a bruise or a black
eye where Billy had mauled him. "Never mind," said his
mother. "Tomorrow you take a nice big piece of cake to Billy,
and he'll be good to you." So the little fellow did as his mother
suggested and gave Billy the cake and Billy ate the cake and
beat up the little fellow again. Sobbingly he explained to his
mother, "Billy wants more cake." And that is the way it goes
when we try to placate evil by mere permissiveness and kindness. That is not the kind of goodness that overcomes evil. The
goodness that overcomes evil is knowledge of spiritual law
and a strong consciousness of spiritual power which flows from
that. For the evil is in ourselves and not in the people who

molest us, and it is in ourselves that the evil must be overcome. The evil is fear, weakness, ignorance, and these always invite their shadows and confirmations. The evildoers in society are the representations of the weaknesses in society. The evildoers in one's personal life come as responses to invitations which one has previously sent out, either voluntarily or involuntarily. These shadows and confirmations cannot move when we have light within. Just as in the animal and in the plant worlds the weaker is always attacked by the stronger, so it is with human beings; when there is poverty of consciousness within, there will be an excess of violence without. Only the strong can be magnanimous and only the rich can be charitable. If one is rich toward God, he can be charitable toward men. Love is the fulfilling of the law not the initiator of its action. When we know the spiritual law and function with it, we are strong in spirit and unafraid of the shadows and the only resultant attitude is charity and good will and inoffensiveness. Thus does love fulfill the law. Spirit is the Father of all things, events, conditions, and relations. The mind that knows this is the only legitimate Son and the Saviour of the world.

This does not excuse the thief or the murderer or the cheat. They are under their own law and it is a law of self-destruction. They kill, steal and cheat because they do not know that "God giveth us all things richly to enjoy," that we possess all things through mind and when we do possess them with the mind, nothing and no one can take them away. When we encounter ugliness, it does not always mean that we ourselves are ugly or if we are robbed it does not mean that we are thieflike. It usually means that we have by carelessness, forgetfulness, or unknowing allowed these occurrences. This law of consciousness has been described by Lao Tze: "I have heard that when the sage goes forth, he carries no spear nor is he afraid of sword or javelin or tooth of rhinoceros for there is in him no place where these may enter."*

---

* *Tao Te Ching,* Stanza 50.

We do not increase life by running from trouble. We do not grow strong by submitting. Slavery only begins when you learn to endure it. Moses led his people out of bondage, and Paul observes that he was able to do this because "he endured as seeing Him who is invisible." He sustained the interior image of what he wanted to do, to be, and to have; and that interior image became his Lord and mastering influence and led him through the wilderness of chaotic human thinking to that promised place of peace and rest for everyone. He endured or persisted in the image of freedom. So let us do.

This chapter has provided a powerful device for increasing your ability to solve problems rapidly and easily. Confront the possible problem mentally before you ever come to it and think out in your mind the words you would say and the actions you would take. Foresee every possible aspect of the problem and prepare your attitude now. What would you do in that case? What would you say in this instance? Prepare your resoluteness, call up your faith, establish your calm, and see yourself as emerging from that situation victorously and happily. Dramatize the whole outcome constructively and joyfully.

The results of this mental course of action are threefold: first, you will save much mental force worrying about troubles which may never arise. You have prepared your course of action and can lay it aside and think no more about that possibility unless and until it arrives. Second, because you have taken the measure of these possible troubles beforehand, you materially cut down their incidence. Few of them will ever come to your door, for your growth and maturity do not require testing by a problem whose measure you have already taken in mind. Third, such problems as do come to you for handling will be dealt with more easily and quickly because you have already been over much of the ground.

This is the happy way of crossing bridges before you come to them.

The Bystanding Mind

Today thousands are trying to "expand the mind" through drugs. Others seek the same end through religious fervor. But euphoria, whether through drugs or through religion, is not mind expansion. The expansion of the sense of *I* comes not through an external agent but through self-realization tested by experience. Apply the great Mind Principle on any matter and note the leverage of your consciousness over that matter, and your sense of *I* has expanded.

Each man's work testifies of his state of mind. It is said that John Singer Sargent, the painter, would never sell a certain canvas of roses which hung on his studio wall. No amount of money would induce him to part with it. He explained, "Whenever I am dispirited, I look at that painting and I say to myself, Sargent, you did that." Meditation and reflection provide insights, reading gives knowledge and inspiration, but only when these are tested against the hard facts of experience and proven productive do we get a better estimate of who and what we are.

Those who take themselves too seriously have not expanded their sense of *I* to include the spiritual and divine part and its magical control over affairs. Their sense of *I* is still confined in arms and legs and cortex. A friend of mine used to advise that one should learn to laugh at himself before 10 o'clock each morning—"You are the funniest thing on earth, anyway." The practice has merit in reducing the false sense of *I*. Surely one of the great sources of unhappiness is in this area of taking ourselves too seriously. Our pride is hurt, our dignity is demeaned, and we are chagrined or insulted. Why? Because our pride is in our human qualities or achievements and not in our divine ones. If we had pride in our divinity, it could not be attacked or hurt, and we should not take ourselves so seriously as to think we *can* be hurt. In case some reader thinks I claim too much for man when I speak of his divinity, I interpret the foregoing thought as follows: The Bible says over and over again that the Creator is one. Logic dictates it. Were there more than one creative power, there would be chaos, for there would be a clash of wills. Now, if you find that your own thought is creative, you have found the One. Your thought is creative not because it is your thought, but because it is Thought. Discover this and you will never again doubt that the presence goes before you.

There is no discovery like self-discovery. When Jacob of old wrestled with his unseen adversary (Gen. 2), his opponent seemed both friend and foe, as every problem or task or challenge does—and is. Unresolved, it can defeat and minimize you. Faced resolutely and carried through, it can bless and enhance you. That the adversary was a messenger of spiritual growth and a means of increased personal worth is indicated by the detail that he wanted to break off the encounter with the coming of dawn. Subjective presences come at night. The fairies and "little people" come out at night and leave with the dawn. These are figurative representations of the truth that when the conscious mind is in abeyance, when cerebration ceases, when one is relaxed and in revery, then subjectivity, intuition, and inspiration are active.

For his persistence in holding out for a blessing, Jacob was rewarded with a new name, or nature. "Thy name shall be called no more Jacob (or John or Joe or Mac) but Israel, which means "a prince ruling with God and with men." In other words, a new sovereignty of will or royally-directed thought is established, and this will and thought govern in the subjective realm of mind and emotions as well as in the objective realm of things and events—with God and with man.

When most modern metaphysicians read the Bible they take the name Israel as referring, not to a religion or a race, but to a certain royal and spiritual state of mind which has all things in its control through knowledge and practice of the governing principle. Having power, it is without fear. Being adequate, it knows no antagonist. Being without opposition or frustration, it is at peace with itself and all the world. The name indicates the true stature and nature of man.

Until the great wrestling match takes place in human experience, the ego or sense of *I* is deficient and naked in a world where all eyes seem to be looking at it. This is not so, but the naked ego feels that it is. When the late Channing Pollock, the playwright, was a child he was taken by his parents to a party. A little girl was present. The children played together until they ran out of ideas, when young Channing said to the girl, "Let's hide behind this curtain and maybe no one will know we are here."

"Maybe no one will care," she replied.

The undeveloped ego feels naked, just as its first parents did in Eden, and strives for a sense of self-importance. When we are not Self-conscious, we are self-conscious. All the egotistical thrusting forward of the self for position, fame, and honor are meager confessions that "I am not all here." This observation brings us back to our interrupted theme of how we humans generally take ourselves much too seriously, having our focus on the outside rather than on the inside.

Great souls, however, will observe that in not taking your human self too seriously you are taking your divine self more seriously. You are considering your spiritual prerogatives and qualities and options and capacities more, and in doing so you are getting outside your personal self and viewing it more objectively, and that means less emotionally, which means, in turn, less vulnerably. For we hurt only when we are identified with littleness, and we are immune to the degree that we are identified with largeness. As Laotse points out, "He who feels punctured, must have been a bubble."*

Correlative to this taking oneself seriously is the bad habit of taking things too personally. Many are always reacting emotionally or taking personally events and situations which are wholly impersonal. I recall a woman who got very angry with the weather man when her car stalled in a big snowdrift, because he had predicted only "snow flurries." By such people any change in situation is resented as a personal affront. A businessman who was retired through the normal procedures of his company spoke of it in personal terms: "They sacked me." A woman, describing a certain encounter, said, "I was livid. I was so furious, I couldn't speak. And when the whole thing was over, I could have kicked myself with shame and felt terribly depressed." Such people are overinvolved; they are too attached, and their feelings have become the prisoners of events. They have not yet learned to stand outside the situation and look at it as a beholder only and not from the angle of a pea in the soup.

Underlying this weakness is the too strong belief that events are causative and not enough awareness that the soul is the arbiter of destiny. By the soul I mean the subjective consciousness of the person. This is the creative factor, and events and circumstances are only verifications or confirmations. Until this is clear to a person, there is little hope of deliverance. When it becomes clear, the terrors and miseries of the world are beating retreat, and fear—ancient enemy of human happiness—is undercut and weakened, and that which has caused millions to tremble is itself trembling. All this because such an awareness puts the Creator back on his throne again in the human mind and heart. Then mind and heart no longer cry out after *the* God, but rather rejoice and exult in *My* God! This

*From *The Way of Life,* Witter Bynner, trans. (New York: John Day Co., 1944), p. 48.

changes the angle, the perspective, and the viewpoint and instead of one being in the middle of a wild vortex of events and crying for help, he is on the outside of what happens to him and around him and views it with a measure of detachment.

So the opposite of all this personal involvement is the detachment of what we are calling here the bystanding mind. This does not imply withdrawal, but rather that we seek to be participants with control. To be a bystander or a beholder, one must stand outside every situation and view it objectively or unemotionally. Why be "livid" at another's remark? Does what he says contribute to your success or failure in any way at all? Yes, he may delude some into thinking ill of you, but does their opinion really make it so? What governs you—your belief or another's? Is the creative cause in another and not in you? Are not all men of one Father or one Source, therefore all sharing the same nature? Why should you make yourself subject to another man's thought? You do it, if you do, only because you have not yet sufficiently respected your own thought. If you knew what thought is, how divine it is, how magical it is, how powerful it is, and if you knew that only your own thought governs you, and not another's, then you would stand up tall and straight and strong in this conviction and fear no other. Persistence in this practice would soon bring out all the truth, and events and accomplishments would prove who and what you are in the eyes of all men. The truth of being is your defense and "against Israel shall not a dog lift his tongue." Another's thought about you has no power unless and until it becomes your thought. Many people spend their days thinking ill of other people but their thought comes to naught, because the people of whom they think do not accept this bad thought and unless they accept, it cannot act. In Wagner's great music-drama, *Parsifal,* the principle of opposition or the adversary or the devil is personified as Klingsor, the evil knight. When he commands the messenger of both good and evil, Kundry, to do his bidding, she rebels and protests and he tells her that he will compel her. She challenges this by saying, "By whose power?" He comes back with this devious but enlightening answer, "Because against my power, your power cannot move." (Act II, Scene I.) In the story of Faust, Mephistopheles is shown to be afraid of the five-pointed star engraved on the floor, for that star is an old symbol of the thinking mind.

Every man is under the governance of his own thought and no other's. Your well-being depends upon your own thought or consciousness, and this principle is the God-in-you or the divine element or Emmanuel of the Bible. It is the only cause. Its government is called the kingdom of heaven. That is why the kingdom of heaven is within you—not as a deposit or a content or an organ, but as a principle of self-government. That also is the reason why the kingdom of heaven "cometh not with observation" as a new society or utopia, which term people often falsely equate with the biblical concept of the kingdom of heaven. The kingdom of heaven comes not by observation but by a change in one's personal psychology. Then outward change follows as a direct consequence. Worship here and you will not be involved there.

That is what the Psalmist counsels: "Only with thine eyes shalt thou *behold* and see the reward of the wicked, but it shall not come nigh thee." This does not mean that you stay out of the fight and refuse to bear your load of the risks and the dangers, but it does mean that you can be freed of the needless consequences of bad thinking and bad action. We are always privileged to take ourselves out of the law of averages and still do our duty. We do not pray that other men should bear our burdens and face our dangers while we go unscathed because of their sacrifice. Rather, we pray that we may do our duty and bear our load and be unhurt.

Undoubtedly each human life has its quota of suffering, but the only purpose and service of suffering is to awaken understanding. With each increase of understanding, the quota of suffering lessens. When a young man goes to war, he may rightly surmise that the risks of his being wounded or killed are very great, and those who love him may feel the same. But this judgment is based upon the law of averages or the human picture only. The more he identifies with the divine element, and the more we who are in prayer for him identify him with that divine element, the less the law of averages operates with him.

To identify with the divine element means to recall the philosophy of the Gita—"water does not wet it, fire does not burn it and swords do not pierce it." When we do this for a man in the war, we are, as I said recently to a father who had two sons in combat, drawing a circle of light around those boys so that it shall not come nigh them. Some weeks later he opened his newspaper and saw a picture of his son and another soldier carrying a wounded comrade off the battlefield. His confidence in the circle of light increased, and it stayed strong until both boys returned home. The more detached one is from the human picture and the human way of judgment, the more identified one is with the divine picture and the more transcendent of human suffering. History is full of instances of those who have so detached and attached themselves that they walked through fire and water and all forms of threatening danger untouched and unhurt.

The practice of being a participating beholder but not an involved pawn of fate consists in looking at all external events and saying with the apostle, "None of these things moves me" (Acts 20). Are you then stony and callous and unfeeling? No! You feel more deeply because you understand, but you do not suffer through overinvolvement. Anyone who thinks at all knows what a burden over-extended sympathy can be. Sympathy means vibrating in unison, so that you suffer all the pains that others suffer and feel deeply the sorrows and miseries of the world. This can go so far as to be practically no help at all. What is needed in such instances is not sympathy but empathy. Empathy means understanding without involvment. Empathy maintains a leverage over the situation, whereas sympathy wallows in it.

Some of the greatest examples of the bystanding mind are

found among the Stoics of Greece and Rome. Listen to this advice from one of them: "Do not suppose you are hurt and your complaint ceases. Cease your complaint and you are not hurt."*

How difficult it is for most of us to cease our complaint! At the human level, men are quite justified in complaining. But complaint indicates that one believes he is hurt. A friend of mine thought he had occasion one day to lay his small son over his knees to spank him. This boy had been taught the difference between events and one's notion of them. As his dad was whaling the boy's posterior, the little fellow turned his face around and laughed in the face of his dad and said, "That hurts the outer man, not me." He had leverage. He had the bystanding mind.

There is an old proverb which says, "Each time the sheep bleats, it loses a mouthful of hay." Cease your complaint, and you strongly imply that you are not hurt. Amplify this implication into understanding that a truly-positioned person cannot be hurt because he is one with the Unhurtable, and immediately you are outside the situation and free and able thereby to improve it and control it.

Very often a person will hold forth on the evils of society and the bad conduct of others. His idealism is great, and he would have all men be as he is. But who made him a judge of anything or anyone but his own life? Let him beware of scorn, disdain or snobbery. Such attitudes are like the bleating of the sheep. They cause one to lose force and dissipate capacity.

Let people be what they want to be or have to be according to their likes—good, bad, or indifferent by your standards. You can disapprove, but do it dispassionately. And let it be said here that this is not "copping out" and letting the world go hang. It is merely putting yourself in a position to be more helpful, more in a position of control.

*Marcus Aurelius, *Meditations,* Jeremy Collier, trans. (London: Walter Scott, Ltd.), Bk. IV, par. 7.

A person has to become exercised over the evils in society or he does not muster the will to try to change them. But when he becomes so exercised as to be bitter of heart, a hater of people, or a despiser of things, then he unfits himself to change things or to be of much help to others. You have to take part in affairs. But the degree of success you have in handling affairs is directly proportionate to the degree of equanimity and moral force you have within. Gandhi called it Satyagrapha, Soul Force. This is why, as Jefferson observed, the democratic process cannot work at its best without education. But the education of the schools is not enough. The Gita points the way: "Firmly seated in yoga, perform action, abandoning attachment . . . and being equal-minded towards success or ill success. Equal-mindedness is called yoga."*

A man confided to me that after half a lifetime of exploding in anger and blowing his top and arguing and fighting, he has "wised up," and now, when faced with a vexatious or explosive situation, he says, "I don't explode and argue; I simply say a little prayer." By this method he keeps his own cool and brings more out of the situation than could otherwise be produced. Another man tells me that his business has multiplied threefold in the last year. He attributes it to the fact that he no longer argues with people in his mind. He attends to his own mental business, and that has prospered his external business.

Here is an executive who has been ten years with his company. He is a good man, but not as good as two or three others at his level of management. He is eager to get ahead and he thinks to further his progress by doing favors and bestowing gifts, especially to his superiors. But always in his mind there is a *quid pro quo*. He expects something in return. He expects those for whom he has done favors to remember him when the promotions come. But they are hard-nosed fellows who judge by performance alone, and he is not promoted. Now he

---

* *The Bhagavad Gita*, Mohini M. Chatterji,trans. (New York: Julian Press, 1960).

is bitter. From what does he suffer? He suffers, not from what others have done or have not done, but rather, from his own opinion of what others ought to have done.

"Take heed that ye do not your alms before men, to be seen of them: otherwise ye have no reward of your Father which is in heaven" (Matt. 6). When you do a kindness, what do you expect? To be noticed and thanked and praised? Or perhaps something in exchange? Then you settle too cheaply. You have your reward, but it is too meager. It satisfies only the human ego and not the sovereign soul. When you settle only for small ends, then you cease to expect and strive for a higher reward from Life itself. Settle for mere ego satisfactions and you lose the thrust and power of self-demand. Make great claims on yourself, for you are great—your individuality opens out into the universal, and from this can come rewards as countless and varied as life itself. The true giver never loses and is never hurt. He gains at every turn. But the giver who gives for a small return not only loses the greater blessing from Life, but his small gift may turn sour. If one is kind and generous by nature, that fact alone commands its own reward, and one need not look to any particular source of reward. If *A* gives to *B*, he may not receive from *B* in return, but may receive from *C* or from *X* or *Y* or *Z*. This is the character of the bystanding mind which beholds the turmoil but has no part in it. Be a beholder. To be a beholder is to be inwardly aloof while outwardly active. As Gandhi once said, Renounce the world, then take it back again on other terms.

When I speak of the bystanding mind, I do not include the bystanding hands. I do not mean quietism without action, unconcern, selfiishness, or irresponsibility. Society has real problems and every citizen owes some effort toward their solution. But his contribution to the general good will be better if he has found his own emotional center of power and peace. The bystanding mind is involved without being embroiled; it is attention without attachment; it is being on top of the job and not having your work ride you. People frequently cry, "Don't just stand there, do something!" The bystanding mind understands this but also values the opposite view: "Don't just do something, stand there!"

Plato stated it boldly and well in *The Republic:* "Until philosophers are kings and the princes of this world have the spirit and power of philosophy and political greatness and wisdom meet in one, cities will never cease from ill—no, nor the human race."

And for any who might think that I place too much emphasis on individual growth and happiness, I offer the view that it is a case of first things first. That Master Mind among men, Jesus, puts the situation thus: "These ought ye to have done, and not to leave the other undone" (Luke 11:42). Moreover, he says, "I pray not for the world, but for them which thou hast given me; for they are thine" (John 17:9). Overconcern for a suffering world is often a projection of one's own need. And many a needy one has helped himself by helping others. Some have become ineffectual nuisances because they did not realize that the main business of living is individual growth, the seeking of the kingdom of heaven which is within. Let one take care of what has been given him—his thoughts, sensations, faculties, judgments, and he will be the best of all help to his fellow men.

Of all the people I know who are serving society, those who are making the greatest contributions in alleviating human ills and wants are those who have themselves in hand. Whether they came to this self-conquest through religion or through their own personal insight and philosophy, they have found an eminence within, which enables them to be towers of strength and sources of inspiration to others.

In a recent writing that came to my desk, I find another example of the way in which people get involved in nonessential considerations. The writer is interpreting the Bible's dietary laws in a purely literal way. He is especially concerned with the prohibition against the eating of swine's flesh. He says that Moses made no mistake in leaving swine out of the list of permitted foods for "he [the swine] was not good from his tail to his snout." The writer waxes poetic regarding our culinary craft with the pig: "We cook him with kraut and boil him with greens, with his mangy old hide we season our beans. We may like him best lean or like him best fat—just as well eat the dog or the mouse or the cat . . . no wonder we are weak and our heartbeats are slow, sanitariums are full, hospitals overflow, for we eat such unclean, abominable things." This writer's theory is an old one, namely, that "we are what we eat." But he takes it at one level only and forgets that "man does not live by bread alone but by every word that proceedeth out of the mouth of God." In other words, we do not live by our physical food alone but by a diet of thoughts and emotions also. He who puts fear into any otherwise healthy article of food is eating of his own fear even if he abstains from that article of food. Scientifically speaking, protein is protein whether it comes from the muscle of a pig or a steer or a rattlesnake.

Of course we are what we eat. But what are we? We are body and mind. The body is composed of substances of the earth and requires a continual replenishment of these for its vitality and health. The mind, with its emotions, is composed of ideas and impressions, and it is healthy and vital when it is continually replenished with inspiration, confidence, hope, wisdom, and understanding. No man lives long without food of the spirit. And it is abundant. "Thou preparest a table before me in the presence of mine enemies." The table of Life is spread right in the midst of turmoil and woe. Every man can eat of new hope and new strength, at will and without leave from any other.

Be a bystander. Don't get overinvolved and thereby invite trouble. Be in all things but not of them. Eat, drink and be merry, not because tomorrow you die but because today you live. And live knowing that it is God that lives in you, and He is Almighty. Your life is the life of God, and that is imperishable, indestructible, free, and unrestrained, transcendent forever.

The Sick Man's Friend

Mary Austin, the novelist, spent a great deal of time living and studying with the Indians of our Southwest. She once witnessed a remarkable healing. A woman of the tribe was sick, but the local medicine man could not relieve her. A famous medicine man from a distant place was summoned. He came and proceeded to build a large fire. When it was blazing, he wrapped the woman in blankets and laid her beside the fire. He went through some ritualistic performances and then lay down beside the woman and apparently went to sleep or into a trance. All night they lay there while others kept the fire going. Just before dawn, the visiting medicine man awoke, stood up, and announced, "I have met the Friend." When full morning came, the woman was well.

To "meet the Friend" for another is to think Truth for him. He is sick and cannot marshal his own thoughts. The healer takes over for him. A rapport is established, which means that the two minds act as one. The healer's clear thought inhibits the patient's erroneous thought and supplants it with Truth. He "suffers not the devils to speak." Because the two minds are in unison, the healer's thought is known in the patient's mind and by repeated emphasis becomes the patient's own thought. Helping another through prayer or what is a technical form of prayer, mental treatment, is much like mountain climbing. The climbers are roped together. If one slips, the others hold on. Or, it is like giving a "firemen's lift" to someone. If he is lame, you throw your arm under his and help him to walk.

But one who is healed in this fashion is not always privy to the means by which it is done, and he may get sick again. He has been helped temporarily—just as when you buy a meal for a hungry man. You have helped him for the moment, but until you show him how to earn his own bread and inspire him to do it, you have not helped him permanently. There are three kinds of help we can give to another: physical, intellectual, and spiritual. Of the three, the second is the most important. You can relieve the distressed spirit by spiritual help. You can remove the discomforts of body by physical means. But only when you teach the mind spiritual wisdom and show it its great prerogative as the middleman between these other two—only then have you set a person's feet permanently upon the path of life.

As a pretty young woman of twenty-three said to me recently: "I have for a long time searched for a way, a place, a religion to find God. Thanks to you I have found him *in me,* because now I know that I am a free spirit and that nothing can belittle me or bind me." As in the healing of Jairus' daughter (Luke 8), "her spirit came again." Why had her spirit departed? Because the mind, the mediator between spirit and body, had accepted many things which were not so, and this had blocked the flow of the spirit.

The process of life is from spirit to mind to body. They are all one. The spirit is life not yet conceptualized, the mind is conceptual life, the body is the manifestation and portrayal of the mind. Each one of us is spirit; that is our identity forever. And spirit is undifferentiated, unconditioned, unconfined, and of infinite potential. It is the province of the mind to measure this undifferentiated spirit and localize and manifest it. When the mind is overburdened with its misinterpretation of environmental impressions, it shuts off its receptivity to the potential of the spirit, and having but a small aperture, allows only a small amount of life to come through. But when the mind is taught to "enlarge the borders of its tent" and "open its windows toward Jerusalem," and at the same time to "fear not them which can kill the body only" (physical things and conditions) but to "fear them which can plunge both body and soul into hell" (thoughts and ideas)—then it becomes master in its own house. Then the mind becomes a mediator between the infinite and undifferentiated world of spirit and the differentiated and finite world of form. In religion the priest has always been called the mediator between God and men: that is what the name means. But the mind is the only true priest, for it is the only mediator between Unformed and formed, or between the Immaterial and the material.

There is another and a better priest than that ordained of men, and a great teacher tells you all about it, if you can read it, in the Book of Hebrews. "After the similitude of Melchisedec there riseth another priest." This priest is Christ, the new mind, the mind redeemed of its delusions born of sense knowledge. As this mind develops in a person, sickness and trouble fall away and wholeness or health manifests. So my young friend, quoted above, has a new measure of herself now and joyfully affirms, "I am all spirit now."

All sickness and indeed all human problems have a generally common origin. They arise from a divided self. Schizophrenia is an extreme example of the pattern. A person is two selves: one that would go and one that opposes the going. He meets the world and is thwarted by it, and frustration mounts. There is in him, as in every person, the drive of the ideal from the spirit side, trying to push through its environment and to manage it. But his conditioned mind closes the doors on the ideal and refuses it entrance. Or argues it to a standstill.

These two selves are to some extent in every person, for

each of us is two things: a spiritual being of dignity and power and a conditioned self made by the world's impressions. That is why we have two fathers—two progenitors or propagators of our life experience. But only one is the true Father. Anything which impresses us is the father of our consequent and subsequent expression. How many impressions of fear and limitation we have gathered since our birth upon this earth and upon this plane! They form a large part of the personality in each and every one of us. This worldly or circumstantial influence is the earthly father which propagates so much limitation and trouble in us.

We are like computers. We get programed and thereafter run automatically. In the course of living, we get a lot of data put into us without our knowledge, and then when some circumstance presses a button, all of the programed data come pouring out. Nothing comes out save what has been put in. But there is this difference with a human being. Our computers were programed originally by Divine Wisdom, and you cannot clear the machine of that original programing. A conflict arises between the divine man who sleeps beneath this earthly self and cries in his idealism for expression: "I am a voice crying in the wilderness, make straight the path of the Lord," and the contrary will which gets built into the mind before the person is aware of what is happening. As the mother in O'Neill's *Long Day's Journey into Night* says, "None of us can help the things that life has done to us. They're all done before you realize it, and when they're done, they make you do other things, until at last everything comes between you and what you'd like to be and you've lost your true self forever."

There is however a reversal. The same law which bound you can release you. That which has been trained can be retrained and that which has been learned can be unlearned. If this principle were not in all life, no animal or man could ever be trained to do anything. After World War I, the famous movie dog Strongheart was taken from Germany, where he had been trained as a vicious fighter and a most efficient killer. This savagery was all trained out of him, and he became instead a noble, lovable, sensitive animal. All things are in each individual; training and education call them out.

The Bible writers refer to these two factors in human consciousness as "the spirit and the flesh." We are counseled to walk not after the flesh but after the spirit. The "flesh" refers to the trained and conditioned part of us, that which has learned to quiver and tremble before events and suggestions of harm. The "flesh" means the habit self which goes on repeating what it has learned until by new thinking it is taught to act differently.

I know a man who listens eagerly for the "pollen count" in the daily news. If the announcer says that the count is high today, he must hurry to take his hay-fever pill as a protection. It would be a new thought to him to suggest that his spiritual nature has sovereignty over the pollen. But should he ever listen to such a thought and accept it, he would then "be led of the spirit" and not be under the law of the flesh.

A person who is dogged by bad luck is "walking after the flesh" because he is following the dictates of habit patterns of thinking which have conditioned him unwittingly. When a nervous, anxiety-ridden man stopped to think about his condition, he recalled a scene from his boyhood which occurred over and over again. After dinner, when the kitchen work was all done, his mother would come into the living room, sit down, smooth out the front of her dress with her hands, and sigh, "Oh my, I wonder where we will all be next year this time!" He recalled that shudders of fear and apprehension moved over him each time he heard her say these words.

A father with a violent temper used to pound the table and shout and threaten the children. The mother, long inured to these explosions, tried to keep peace by cautioning the children to remain silent and do nothing to provoke their father. But deep inside, reflexive nervous patterns were being established, and long after the father's voice was still, the flesh of grown-up men and women would tremble unaccountably.

These are all examples of what it means to "walk after the flesh." What a pity that so many have been taught that these expressions of Paul refer only to sex and what has been called carnality, with connotations of immorality. The flesh or the body is the re-presentation of the mind and its emotions. The emotions are the driving force of the personality, and when once set going they tend to go on mechanically and automatically, forcing the individual to do what he would not. Paul was a great psychologist who early discovered the law of emotional compulsion: "I find then a law that, when I would do good, evil is present with me. For I delight in the law of God after the inward man, but I see another law in my members warring against the law of my mind and bringing me into captivity of the law of sin which is in my members" (Rom. 8). But he also discovered a way out of this conflict and impasse. That way was to "walk after the spirit"—to listen to the pure voice of the spirit within, which always whispers of hope and confidence, which guides and instructs and inspires, which urges and stimulates, kindles desires and wakens enterprise. To walk after the spirit means to listen and to believe that God does not mock when he sends us the heart's true desire. To walk after the spirit means to accept the desire as the promise of God, to believe that that which sends the desire will also send the fulfillment. Then, just as one was formerly compelled into anxiety and trouble, so he will now be compelled into peace and good fortune. Those who are led of the spirit become sons of God or the expression and manifestation of the highest and the best.

God made no sick man. Whence then comes sickness? Some will say, from our false beliefs. What is a belief? A state of mind. And with that answer we are back with our basic principle: there is only one power of creation; the Creator must be one. If we find the creator power anywhere, we have found the One. And we have just found it in a negative state of mind or a false belief! Consciousness is creative of both good and bad. Good thought makes good things. Bad thought makes bad things. All thought is creative.

This discovery knocks out another shibboleth of religious thought: that God is total good. This concept has given rise to a great deal of tension and may often make more sickness than it cures or prevents. For if the Making Power is all good, whence comes the evil? And the answer is that evil does not originate with another power than God, but is the result of the limited use of the one power. Let us go back to the form of the mind as an aperture or doorway between the Inexhaustible and Perfect Spirit on one side and manifestation and experience on the other. When the doorway is small, only a small amount of life comes through. Let Perfection be represented by 100 units. Anything less than that is evil to the degree that anything less than perfection is disturbing or hurtful.

Let's make no mistake here. The Spirit is perfect, but when mind, the middleman, measures too little, that little is experienced as evil. We are perfect spiritually and whenever we remember this we are improving our mind by enlarging its concept. All we are is what we know, and we may know a disastrous wrong. Dr. Quimby said: "All the world believes a lie, so when I tell it the truth it thinks I am telling it a lie." The truth he told is that the true man is adequate and capable and perfect in all his ways. The world mind believes that there are many things and powers that can make one sick apart from knowing it. That is the lie. There is but one power of causation and creation. It is consciousness. That is God or the Making Power in the life of man. "For though there be that are called gods, whether in heaven or in earth (as there be gods many and lords many), but to us there is but one God, the Father of whom are all things and we are in him" (1 Cor. 8).

In this antiseptic and prophylactic age, millions are afraid of germs. But there is abundant evidence that germs do not cause disease—fear does, false knowing does. Henry Bieler, M.D. in his excellent book, *Food Is Your Best Medicine,* says, "I came to the conclusion that germs do not *initiate* a diseased state of

the body but appear later after a person becomes ill."* Many
other physicians have come to a similar conclusion. Germs
appeared *after* the dis-ease has been first set up by fear or
anxiety or rage or envy or a medley of unworthy emotions.

A man attended the lectures of a colleague of mine in carpet
slippers. He had arthritis. For nine years he had suffered. He
was told that he must change his thinking in order to change
his dour state of mind. He came for a private consultation and
related that his trouble had started during a time of financial
reversal. A doctor told him that his trouble was due to fear and
that he never would get over it until he lost his fear. "But"
the patient said, "I am all over that now. I have confidence and
can get along all right, but I have this physical trouble." The
teacher asked him *why he felt that he must have arthritis.* He saw
no reason. After some further prompting, he said, "I am going
to tell you what I have never told anyone, not even my wife."
He had taken some money. He felt guilty. He felt that his
illness was coming to him. The teacher then asked "Why don't
you forgive yourself?" He could not understand that. They
read Matthew 9 together, including these words: "Thy sins are
forgiven thee."

At first our man objected, as many have, that only Jesus
could forgive sin, and in this particular instance it was the man
in the Bible who was forgiven and not all men in general. This
attitude not only shows the tendency of the negatively-condi-
tioned human mind, always seeking arguments against itself,
but is the very stock in trade of priestcraft throughout the ages:
only certain special or ordained persons can forgive sin. Jesus
taught none of this. By his words and example he demon-
strates that forgiveness is inherent in the nature of things. The
universe holds no grudges. The Life Principle does not judge,
and knows no good or bad. Good and bad are relative terms
of human judgment based on imperfect knowing. The universe is not capricious. The sun shines and the rain falls on the

*New York: Random House, 1965, p. 39.

just and the unjust. The law of gravity doesn't know any difference between a good man and a bad one. Electricity does not discriminate. It will power the machine that fashions a safe and will turn the drill of the burglar who robs it. And if sickness betokens sin and sin is due to a wrong concept—and if changing the concept cures the sickness—then any man has power to forgive his own sins. Forgiveness is an exchange of opinion. You give up or give over an old and limiting opinion in exchange for a better or more expansive one.

The man with arthritis began to see all this. He began to see that forgiveness was in his own power. He saw that he was sick because he felt unworthy of being well. He saw that he was not being punished for his error, but was punishing himself by his feeling of unworthiness. Being an honest man now, he was not the same man who stole the money. And even the civil law does not put a man twice in jeopardy for the same crime. He saw that when Jesus told the woman, "Thy faith hath saved thee," and the blind man, "According to your faith be it unto you," he was declaring that forgiveness was theirs in the moment of insight by right of a change of consciousness in themselves and not by the leave of another. For years this man had done no work. The next week he worked every day, all week!

God wants no man to be sick. "In Zion [the transcendent state of mind] the inhabitant shall not say I am sick; the people that dwell therein shall be forgiven their iniquity." All provision has been made for our personal health and happiness in the nature of things. All that remains is the knowing of it, the opening of the aperture to let the light come through.

How do we do this? Forgive yourself. Forgive others. Withhold judgment. The Father or Life forgives us *as* we forgive others and ourselves. That is, the Source will ease your hurt only when you give up your need to be hurt. Then proceed to accept yourself as you are in truth, as you were made, as you are in God. Accept your divine prerogative. Accept your spiritual being, perfect in all its parts and nature. Coerce your mind to accept this truth. For only when you love yourself will you or can you love others.

And if someone should not see the necessity of the eleventh commandment to "love others as I have loved you," let him be reminded that love is the fulfilling of the law.

The case is similar with sacrifice. We have been taught that sacrifice is giving up something dear, and that makes for nobility of spirit and the grace of God. But that is nonsense. Many a mother has sacrificed all for her children and saved nothing of herself. She becomes in the end, as Prentice Mulford once observed, a derelict over which the children walk to their own ends. And many a daughter and often a son has sacrificed his or her life for the parents. If such a sacrifice brings peace and satisfaction, all is well. But often it brings only bitterness.

Here, for example is a woman of forty-five, still loyal to her parents but eating her heart out at the unfairness of it all. Her sisters and brothers have married long ago and have homes and children to rejoice in. This woman's emotional accent and energy are geared to depression, resentment, emptiness, and inward revolt. She is religious and she prays a good deal. But she is often resentful of God and wonders why he does not deliver her. She wonders why men say that God is just. If God is just, why does he allow this terrible unfairness? There is little grace or nobility in this woman's sacrifice.

True sacrificial living and giving ends always in the enhancement and enlargement of a person. Because there is an exchange of values. Sacrifice is noble, but it is also selfish. Mark Twain illustrates: You are about to catch a trolley late at night in a cold and snowy blizzard. Your home is far out and you have just enough money for your fare. You notice an old woman with a bundle, walking. You know that she also lives a great distance away and that she is walking because she has no money, or so little that she wants to save it for food. You go up to the woman and say, "Here mother, please take this and ride home tonight." Then you walk home, mile after mile in the howling storm. But your heart is light! A lovely feeling warms you and satisfies you. You sacrificed and you are glad! Mark Twain says that you were selfish—you wanted that feeling of having done a good turn and you gave your last penny in exchange for it. There was nothing noble about it. It was a transaction in consciousness—a fair exchange.

When the bases are loaded, the batter bunts. He is put out at first, but the runner at third comes home. That is called a sacrifice hit. Sacrifice, like forgiveness, is an exchange of the lesser for the greater. If you have the mind and tendency of a scholar, run down the meaning of the words *sacrifice* and *sacred* back to their roots and you will have a revelation.

The law of Life provides for every good and happiness. The law is belief, faith, opinion, consciousness. As you think, so you are and so you act. Every thought authorizes some action. There is no action without its corresponding thought. That, by the way, is the meaning of meta-physics in the modern sense. The preposition, *meta* means "accompanying." Among prepositions, its meaning is midway between *to* and *from*. Every physical expression has an originating and presiding *meta*. To remove the physical, you must attend to the *meta,* the unseen, immaterial reality which accompanies the physical. The physical is the shadow cast by an inward light—even if that light be darkness.

Love yourself, for you are "fearfully and wonderfully made." Love yourself because you come from a divine source.

Your Luck-Line

No game is ever lost until it is lost in the mind. That is a truism. In what way is it true? Imagine the worst reversal that could come to you. So long as you have not lost your reason and still have your disposing mind, the essential you is not hurt. So long as you can make a distinction between yourself and what has happened to you, you are above the trouble. Part of you would cry out in protest, to be sure: "But my business is gone, my home is gone, my debts are more than I can pay, and you say I am not hurt!" I do! Your affairs are hurt; your state of mind is altered. But your mind is not hurt. Behind your state of mind is your whole mind, and behind your mind is the Universal Mind, and Mind is the God of all worlds, including yours.

"See I have made thee a god to Pharaoh" (Exod. 7). In the Bible scheme Pharaoh represents the phenomenal world; subjectivity (Moses) is its god. In spite of your trouble, then, you are untouched in your essential and sovereign nature. You still have the most prized possession, the only force that can ever achieve anything or ever allowed anything to be achieved— your power of choosing how you shall think of any situation. All that is required of a man is that he do justly, love mercy, and walk humbly with his God (Mic. 6). You can still do this, so you are in no way diminished, hindered, or restrained. And since wealth and success are matters of consciousness, you have lost only temporarily and may rebuild at will. "Destroy this temple [of consciousness] and in three days I will raise it up" (John 2).

The foregoing is a large part of the way the mind thinks when it gives a spiritual mind treatment for alleviation of any difficulty or the solution of any problem. Don't try to improve the situation by thinking, however positively, about it. This will only succeed in involving the mind more in the intricacies of the problem. Instead, turn the mind to consideration of its prerogative. Think how spiritual man is always in dominion, that the true man is free and never was in bondage to any person, place, or thing. "Whom he did foreknow, he also did predestinate" (Rom. 8).

As F. L. Rawson, the great English metaphysician, used to advise when engaging in spiritual treatment, don't think of material good. To do so is to drop the mind down into the welter of contrary suggestions. Think rather, of immaterial good. Rehearse in your mind all the highest truths you know. Recall scriptures which are meaningful to you, and such axiomatic statements as these: "There is nothing good or bad, but thinking makes it so." "It is not what happens to you, but what you think of what happens to you, that makes the difference between happiness and misery." "Every thought tends toward its own embodiment." "Every thought is nascent action." "You have nothing to deal with but your thought." "Let your opinion lie still and you do not suffer."

Don't treat or try to improve the situation by your thinking. Use no force or will power. "In any contest between the will and the imagination, the imagination will always win." The mind is a mirror and always reflects what it is turned to; turn it to the divine truth. Let this be your only voluntary action, and the involuntary action of the mind at its deeper levels will change the situation. When blocked horizontally, rise vertically. I have called this the helicopter technique of surmounting the anxiety produced by a situation. "Look unto the hills (the spiritual truths) from whence cometh your help." "Flee to the mountains"—the highest insight. Go to chapters forty to forty-five of Isaiah and read such statements as these: "I, even I, am the Lord and beside me there is no saviour . . . I am the first and I am the last and beside me there is no god . . . I am the Lord and there is none else, there is no god beside me . . . I am the Lord: that is my name and my glory will I not give to another." Think on these absolutes until the mind itself becomes absolute and ceases its debate. Then the mind rests, and it "rests in the Lord," the executive will of life, ordaining more life and health and happiness in abundance.

Sometimes it is advised, "Take no thought," for "which of you by taking thought can add one cubit to his stature?" But the application of these words is frequently erroneous and confusing. The Master does not downgrade thinking or suggest that the thoughts in the mind are not creative, that there is no profit or efficacy in right thinking. What he does say is this: Take no thought (and the context tells us that he means no worrisome thought), for it should be obvious that to think about nothing at all would be to become like a vegetable or a stone. Besides, you cannot think of nothing. The mind is thinking all the time. It is communicating with an objective world and a subjective world and receiving impressions from both. What it does with these impressions is its life.

The only life you have or know is your kind. The mind is a spot of light between two darknesses. Without the mind there is no life, consciousness, or awareness—for all these terms are generally synonymous. Take thought about life, then, and not about its processes and manifestations. For if the life be healthy, the manifestations will come along as its active re-presentation.

We are told to "let this mind be in you, which was also in Christ Jesus" (Phil. 2). What is the mind that was in Christ Jesus? It must be a mind far above and beyond the ordinary, average mind which Jesus called the world ("in the world, ye shall have tribulation, but be of good cheer; I have overcome the world") (John 16). The Master Mind is that mind which leaves the world and goes to the Father, not as a final act of the body but as a daily act of the mind. Leaving the world and going to the Father is the highest method of prayer. It is turning the mirror of the mind away from vexation and confusion of the outer scene and considering the great truths of being until the mind becomes composed, authoritative, and creative of divine order and divine right action in the affairs of men. Such a mind is the kingdom of God, the government of God, the will of God being done on earth in material form and process, as it always is in heaven, the realm of principle and prototype.

So don't be overly concerned about your material needs and ambitions before you have been primarily concerned with establishing the state of mind which alone can make these material goods what you want them to be. "After all these things [material wants, ambitions, eating and drinking, and getting ahead] do the Gentiles seek." The Gentiles are those minds which are outside of the law—outside the understanding of spiritual law. But that mind which was in Christ Jesus is the mind of Israel, the spiritual mind, which I have touched on in a previous chapter.

Right thinking is not to be understood as merely indulging in optimistic sayings, making positive statements in the midst of tremulous feelings, or affirming that everything is all right when one is in the midst of difficulties. We need not tell lies to ourselves. This only compounds the conflict and the confusion. If this kind of thinking is what is meant by those who say that thinking does not do it, that neither right thinking nor wrong thinking is a power, then of course they are quite right. But let us above all things strive to be clear. It is the devil that confuses. Christ gives light.

There is one great denial and there is one great affirmation. Deny that any person, place or thing, any situation, circumstance, suggestion, or baneful prophecy can, in and of itself, do anything to bless or to harm you. This dissipates fear as a strong wind dissipates a fog. It tends to undercut all subconscious feelings of negation and "suffers not the devils to speak."

Immediately upon the heels of this denial comes the affirmation that God is the only power and by this is meant that the spirit and the mind of a person, which are God localized, are the only creative factor in the person's life. There is no other. "My glory I do not give to another." If the mind doubts, challenge it to find another. "Produce your cause, sayeth the Lord; bring forth your strong reasons, sayeth the King of Jacob" (Isa. 4). After this basic and preliminary work has been done, then one may proceed to the lesser affirmations and denials and they will be effective. In the words of the great Stoic emperor: "Does what has befallen thee hinder thee one whit from being just, highminded, chaste, sensible, deliberate, straight forward, modest, free and from possessing all the other qualities, the presence of which enables a man's nature to come fully into its own? Forget not in future, when anything would lead thee to feel hurt, to take thy stand upon this axiom: This is not misfortune, but to bear it nobly is good fortune"*

This brings us back to the main theme of the present chapter, which is how to be more fortunate in one's affairs. We all know that there are *lucky* and *unlucky* people, and it is often a mystery why they are what they are. Here is an example of what is called *good luck*. A farmer tells it: "A fellow came up to the house last January and said that his car was stuck in the snow. My son and I went to give him a hand. We got to talking and he said he was the manager of a new store in town. He said he was going to open up a farm-equipment department. It just happened that my son was looking for a job and this was right down his line. It worked out fine. He started as a salesman, and now he is managing the department. A. H. Z. Carr

*Marcus Aurelius, *Meditations*, Jeremy Collier, trans. (London: Walter Scott Ltd.), Bk. IV, par. 49.

gave this illustration in a book whose philosophy was: Expose yourself, get yourself ready for the big break when it comes. This story is an example of what is called good luck. Mr. Carr called it the *luck-line,* which is thought of as an invisible thread of awareness between ourselves and all others who cross our path. The more such lines a person throws out, the more luck he is likely to have. Every encounter, every situation, every chance meeting holds some possibility, and a lucky person becomes aware of it and profits by it. The lucky person consciously or unconsciously follows the biblical instruction and "despises not the day of small things," for to him every situation is an opportunity. His luck-line is out on all occasions and in all situations. He knows that "all things work together for good" to those whose luck-line is out.

Now, we can imagine what some people in an older way of thinking would say. Be good, do good, be kind and helpful, and life will see your goodness and reward you. But you and I know that things do not always work out this way. All kind and helpful people are not lucky. Some of them are miserably unlucky. Sometimes, as scripture says, "the wicked flourish like the green bay tree." Quite often people who are not good by religious or ethical standards seem to prosper better than those who are conventionally good. The Psalmist frequently warns us not to fret because of evildoers; but we cannot avoid fretting ourselves because of evildoers if we do not know our own spiritual powers, and thus do not spin our luck-line according to spiritual principle. Those who still think that if they help older people with their bags, get early to the office, and work late, they will prosper are moving headlong into disappointment unless they add the spiritual dimension to that philosophy. In today's world, promotion does not always come because of virtue or strength, or even industry.

Being "good" is not sufficient. We have all seen "good" people go out of their way to be helpful, only to reap misfortune. Years ago I heard of just such a one. He was a prosperous businessman and a good man. He lost his business and his wealth, and in trying to recoup turned to ranching. First his cow died, then his mule. The wind blew down his windmill. He got discouraged and moved to the city. He broke his nose, then three ribs and a collarbone. Later his leg was paralyzed because of a splinter of glass. Then his father and his mother became seriously ill, and to cap it all his wife had a dog that bit him whenever she told it to. All this he related to the judge when he was arrested by police who came to get him away from his wife. They found him in bed trying to comfort himself with a bottle of liquor. They took him to jail, and even in jail he was not safe because someone slammed the door on his hand and broke three fingers. Today, psychology would say that that man was "accident-prone." In ordinary terms, we would say he was just plain unlucky even though he was good. The judge was moved to tears when he heard this tale and fined him one hundred dollars and suspended the fine. There are thousands who have a bad luck-line, and out of every experience they draw only some misfortune or loss.

On the other hand, there are people who are success-prone and safety-prone. No matter where you put them, in danger or in challenge, they extract some good from the experience. An old proverb says of such a person, "Throw him into the water and he will come up with a fish in his mouth." No matter where you put him or what you do to him, he will turn it to account. He will take profit from any circumstance. That is exactly the teaching of the ancient Stoics: if a man is truly lucky in the highest sense, he will turn any situation to good account. Is this bad fortune which has befallen me? So it is bad fortune. Does that deprive me of my capacity to bear it nobly? It does not, and in that fact is good fortune.

Stoicism in our time has fallen into some kind of disrepute. The modern mind tends to think of the Stoic as indifferent to pleasure or pain, someone who has practiced such indifference that he is untroubled by sensation of any kind. The old story of the Spartan youth who stole a fox and hid it under his shirt illustrates somewhat the way the modern thinks of Stoicism.

When the youth was in danger of being caught, he let the fox gnaw at his vitals rather than utter a sound. The true Stoics were not those who withstood great pain or great adversity only. They were men who did something about their adversity by doing something within and upon themselves.

Modern metaphysical teaching emphasizes the same truth. There is always something you can do about everything, and that something is in your thought. You are never in any situation, no matter how bad it looks or feels, that you cannot modify by your attitude and even take some profit from. This may not be readily apparent, and it may not prove itself for weeks or months, or maybe years, but if you think and act in a certain way while you are in any predicament, it will turn that predicament to good account for you. That kind of thinking, practiced until it becomes second nature, establishes what we call the luck-line.

There is a Universal Mind in which our private minds exist as operating centers, and this Universal Mind knows all things and is everywhere present, all the time. This Universal Mind is in us and we are in it, so if our luck-line is out, and if we make constant reference to the fact that through Universal Mind we are in touch with all people and with all things, then we are in touch with our good, even though we do not presently recognize it. Thus we learn to think and act in such a way as to capitalize on any event. If one is lucky in this sense, all situations are opportunities.

A good example is the late Graham McNamee and the way he became a great announcer in the early days of radio. He was on jury duty in lower New York one day. During a recess he looked out the window and noticed a sign being put up on a building across the street. It had four meaningless letters on it. Curious, he learned from workmen that they were the call letters of a broadcasting station. He knew nothing about radio, but it occurred to him that they might have use for a singer. He spoke to the manager. The answer was a curt, "No." McNamee accepted the refusal good-naturedly and

asked about the mechanics of the new business. At this display
of interest the manager said that he was going into the control
room presently, would McNamee care to see what it looked
like? He would, indeed! After their tour of the station, the
manager remarked that McNamee had a good speaking voice.
They might need another announcer. Perhaps he would care
to make a voice test. In ten minutes the test was made and in
ten more minutes McNamee was hired and a notable radio
career was launched.

Notice how McNamee extended his luck-line. Through attention and interest he broadened his consciousness by becoming aware of new facts and opportunities. He went along with
present events and did not resent them or grow despairing.
He opened himself and learned about a new development.
We cannot sit still and wait to be discovered. The lucky person
pushes out in thought and action. A dozen other men in that
same situation would not have been hired, even though they
had the same good speaking voice and the same kind of personality and all the other qualities except one: the attitude
hidden in the heart.

That attitude may be there by nature as it was in McNamee,
or it may be established by constant reference to oneself as an
expression of the Oversoul and therefore equipped for every
occasion, made to win and therefore lucky. One cannot expect
specific rewards for specific acts; one should rather enlarge his
view to expect his reward from Life itself. If one derives from
that story of the farmer and his son only the idea that just
because this boy was good and helpful he was rewarded, this
would be a grievous mistake. We are not always rewarded for
specific acts. To expect it and then be disappointed when it
does not materialize is to shorten the luck-line and to carry
unnecessary psychic burdens, as I have already pointed out.
Our good does not always return to us from the same quarter
on which we have expended effort. We learn to invest in life,
and we put our trust in the law of consciousness, and if one
has the consciousness of victory and luck, then it makes no

difference where you put him. Add an understanding of the law of consciousness to your philosophy and you have a spiritual strength and a dimension to your thought which will tend to make you lucky. Things and people and situations and events are not the cause of our happiness or our misery, but we give them power in our ignorance. In the silence of your own soul withdraw this power from others and from things and stake out your claim in the land of consciousness. What you claim in consciousness, nobody can deny you. This gives force and quality to thought and purpose and vitality to action. It leads to the realization of Walt Whitman, "I, myself, am good fortune." Moreover, it voids anger and bitterness and resentful feelings, all of which rob men of their strength.

One who stakes his claim there in this area of wisdom and realization is said in the Bible to have rested in the Lord or the Law. "Rest in the Lord and do good and verily he shall give thee the desires of thine heart." Again, the Psalmist counsels, "Fret not thyself because of evil-doers." Do not allow fretfulness to rob you of the energy which, if expended positively, would take you to victory and happiness and peace. This gives a kind of muscle tone to the thought, a sense of the inevitability of good luck. It makes for what is called among practical people great presence of mind.

Mind is everywhere. Everything is full of the presence of Infinite Mind. You are in it, I am in it. It is in us. All of everything is where we are. The trick is to keep tuned into this universal fact and therefore to feel accoutered and equipped for every occasion, adequate in every situation, because of the infinite resources of being. There is one Being, call it whatever you wish, and you are one with it, inseparable. Emerson says, "The Oversoul had need of an organ where I am, else I would not be here." A friend of mine used to add to this the words, "therefore God is my instant and everlasting support." You are the organ of an infinite wisdom and power.

Since that is so, who is it that goes to work in the morning, who is it that meets the challenges of the day, who is it that faces trouble or limitation of any kind? Answer these questions correctly to yourself and your luck-line is out. Thinking of yourself in terms of this larger identity, you cannot be defeated or withheld in the accomplishment of any true aim. The Infinite cannot be denied. Think in this way and you are in the luck-stream immediately, and for you there are fish in any kind of water.

When the private mind is open to this dimension of being, then the individual has greater presence of mind, for more of the Universal Mind is available for his needs and purposes. Years ago one of our great airlines instituted a school for stewardesses. Presence of mind was one of the first qualities they looked for in the young women who have since done such a wonderful job on our airlines. Their alertness, comprehension and awareness are responsible for much of the success of air travel. Presence of mind is really the presence of God. Wherever we see good presence of mind in a human being we see a greater availability of infinite wisdom and awareness than in the average individual. The more presence of mind there is in any situation, the more right action governs that situation.

From "Have To" to "Want To"

In these two phrases we describe lucky and unlucky persons. The difference between them is the difference between misery and happiness. "Have to" is an obligation. "Want to" is freedom. One is a necessity and a burden. The other is a luxury and agreeable. "Have to" people are driven by their desires, their needs, duties, debts, jobs, bosses, and society with all its pressures. "Want to" minds are not driven, but rather drive. Like a sailing vessel, they take advantage of every wind that blows. Even when the wind is contrary, they make use of it to take them where they want to go.

Consider the sad plight of the migrant workers who pick our fruits and vegetables from the Mexican to the Canadian border. We often hear with indignation of the deplorable conditions under which they live and the meager wages they earn. But this is not all the fault of society or of those who hire them. One mother of six was interviewed recently and said that when she was a little girl her mother told her that they were poor and that no matter how hard she tried, they would always be poor. She went on, "You know what? She was right. That is why I do not kill myself working, it is not worth it." She was a genial soul and had adapted to her environment and her condition in life. But she had never considered how her mother's thought had placed her in bondage and restricted her outlook on life. She was a slave to the most tyrannical of masters, *small thought.* Yet she did have one small but great possession—her geniality and good feeling.

As we have observed, this good feeling when mixed with but a little faith, will do wonders. This migrant mother had what a certain other "woman of the wives of the sons of the prophets" had (2 Kings 4), when she went to Elisha saying, "Thy servant, my husband, is dead; and thou knowest that thy servant did fear the Lord and the creditor is come to take unto him my two sons to be bondmen." All she had in the house was a pot of oil. Oil always indicates a happy spirit or a mood of geniality. The prophet told her to go "borrow thee vessels abroad of all thy neighbors, even empty vessels, borrow not a few" and then pour out the oil into all those vessels. And then the flow of the oil stopped. What does the old story tell us in terms of our psychology and our way of living? There is none so poor who does not have hidden beneath the poverty of his life a little bit of gladness and buoyancy. In fact, the poor often have more of a sense of humor than the rich. They have to.

Let the poor woman use what she has. Let her put it to work. Have her pour out what little spirit she has into vessels or concepts that enlarge her thought. Since she does not possess any concepts of enlargement, let her borrow some. If she has no courage, let her borrow the attitude of courage. History is full of examples. If she has no confidence, let her borrow it by watching those who have. If she has no sense of security, let her borrow the thought that God is her security, and walk in it until it becomes her own. "Act as though I were and ye shall know I am."

We own nothing in this world. We have borrowed everything we have. We came into this life naked in body and mind. The first thought we had, like the first garment, belonged to another. A man often walks over the acres of his estate or considers the amount of his wealth and feels a glow of pride that whispers, "All this and this and this is mine." It is not. He is only a steward of his possessions, a tenant on his land, and a guest at the table of time. All that we are and all that we have are matters of consciousness. To get more, one must be more. What one does not own, one can borrow and use until he makes it his own. When he has made it his own, he has magnified and increased it, and others will borrow from him.

If you wish to move from "have to" to "want to," keep your geniality. As I have indicated earlier, "faith worketh by love," and in the presence of good feeling all things work together for good. A person may have all the talent in the world, all the know-how, be highly endowed and have highly developed skills, have learned so much that he is a walking encyclopedia, but if he cannot put all that into good feeling and use it with geniality, then there is poverty within and without.

If you look at all the scientific evaluations which have been made of the causes that make people fail or succeed, you will find over and over again that the element that causes the most failure is not lack of talent or ability, or a lack of education or experience either, but rather a lack of personality adjustment. It is the failure to find an opulent area of good feeling within oneself and to be able to communicate and exchange it with others of similar disposition. People fail when they cannot get along with other people. Other people rub them the wrong way, or their ego gets in the way. It is this lack of good feeling within that puts people in the "have to" class where they feel driven by life and circumstance. The "more excellent way" which Paul points to in his sublime chapter is the way that the "want to" folks take. They drive but are not driven. They love work, they rejoice in challenges and in shouldering responsibility.

Often a person who starts with little in life seems to get this drive better than the person who starts with much. That is why so many of our East Side boys have distinguished themselves.

Al Jolson and Al Smith started in poverty, and that very poverty sparked their desires and their efforts. So many of our great achievers are those who develop drive out of their privation and make their inferiority an impetus. To jump high one must often crouch low. Don't be afraid of your inferiority or your lowliness. Used correctly, it can be a great stimulus to higher achievement. It can be a help in moving from "I have to" to "I want to."

Religion announces goals and lays down moral laws for the attainment of the good life. But modern man has found that this is not sufficient. Those who have kept the moral laws religiously are not always more successful, healthier, or happier than those who have neglected this practice. Many a person who has not stolen, has not killed, has not gossiped about his neighbor, has kept the Sabbath and honored his father and mother and accepted Christ as his savior, may still find life a drudgery, his body subject to ills, and his affairs to misfortune. Something more is required. There is a mental law that we can use to get the subconscious going for us rather than against us.

Matthew Arnold gives us a clue as to how it is done. "We cannot kindle when we will, the fire that in the heart resides. But tasks in hours of insight will'd, can be through hours of gloom fulfill'd." Would it not be wonderful to be able so to affect your own subconscious in a moment of insight—in a moment when your spirit is high and your perception clear—as to give it an order to be performed subsequently, something like a posthypnotic suggestion? There is just such a practice and such a technique, and the poet knew it. Tasks in hours of insight willed can be in moments of gloom fulfilled.

Most of us wait until we are sick before we pray for help. Most of us wait until the cupboard is empty before we pray for substance. Most of us wait until we get into trouble before we start to use our knowledge and to marshal our powers. The law I am speaking of here is just opposite of this practice. Pray when you are not in need, so that you will be skillful and relaxed in your technique and not under pressure when need comes. When you are relaxed and well and happy, think definitely why you can confidently expect always to be so. Project the image of your well-being into the future and accept it for all time. Invoke the blessing of the Most High for all time. Think of how you want always to be in divine law and order and have right action taking place in the whole of your life. Think of yourself as going from strength to strength and from knowledge to knowledge and from joy to joy. And if doubt challenges your mind in such a moment of meditation, argue it down by pointing out to yourself that the law of all things is consciousness, and "as a man thinketh in his heart so is he."

Remind yourself that the Word is God (John 1), that every thought tends toward its own embodiment, and your thought is powerful and clear in this regard, not merely because it is your thought but because all thought has this characteristic and power, and yours is no exception. Point out to yourself that every man carries his reward and his punishment within his own thought, and since you have chosen good thought, then good thought is ruling and governing in you and establishing in mind what shall hereafter appear as fact and function and experience. Strengthen yourself in all these insights, declarations, projections, and realizations. That is self-treatment; that is using what you have. You will find, as these treatments take hold in the subconscious, that you are being guided and directed more than before. You will find that when you seem to be weakest, you will be strongest. You will discover that right action is more habitual, that even when you can't think positively or see your way clearly, something in you is activating you and even compelling you to say the right word, do the right thing, walk in the right direction. There is a charm upon you and about you. Your wish is your will, and what you do is done without struggle and debate. This takes you out of that burdensome, onerous, slavelike existence. It brings you into the class described by the phrase "want to." All your inclinations, desires, and automatic, habitual movements seem to go unerringly in the direction of livingness.

Another great step in moving from "have to" to "want to" is in recognizing that every job and occupation is a symbol of the real job we all have to do. The real job is realizing and becoming aware of ourselves as spiritually free beings without the necessity of struggle and fear. Spiritual man was given dominion in the beginning (Gen. 1), and all our pilgrimage through the world of matter is to reawaken this awareness.

Every job in the world is simply a struggle to get order out of chaos, coherence out of incoherence, and wisdom out of ignorance. Every time we do a piece of work well, we learn something new about ourselves. A laborer, a housewife, a writer, and an artist are all doing exactly the same thing from the point of view of the subjective self. They are learning about themselves. Did you ever notice how parents learn from their children? A little angel is born into a household and casts its charm and redeeming effect over all the house. Parents also see their own bad habits dramatically reproduced in their children, and this has a favorable reaction upon their own growth. Many a person says in his later years, "If I had my life to live over again, I would do thus and thus." This shows that he has learned something from the passing years. This life is a school in which we prepare for the higher grades. No job is as onerous with this recognition as it was without it. Knowing that our real job is building confidence and character and awareness and insight, we can work on in any situation and know that we are making a profit above and beyond our wages.

In every job we are imposing our will upon the chaos of unformed matter just as God did in the beginning when he looked upon the earth and it was chaotic and without form, and he reacted in terms of a definite decision to make something orderly out of it (Gen. 1). Think of a writer who is trying to articulate an idea. He is trying to bring lucidity out of the confusion of his thoughts. His world is without form and void, and he is advancing upon the chaos and the darkness with every insight at his command. A carpenter takes the wood of a tree and out of it fashions a cabinet of beauty and utility. He has imposed his will upon the unformed matter. And in doing this he has learned something about himself, for he can say as Sargent said about his roses, "I did that."

This is what we call growth in consciousness and awareness. It is soul growth. All our labor upon this earth is for this purpose and this purpose only. Whether we think or teach or construct or buy or sell, all our effort is to attain to self-realization and self-discovery. As it is in heaven, so shall it be known on earth.

We save ourselves an immense load of vexation and care when we know this, for then it is a matter of some indifference what job we are engaged in. We may have talent and skill in banking, in merchandising, in science, or in the arts, but whatever it is, it is only incidental to our real job, which is self-unfoldment. Thus everyone can make progress where he is, even if he is doing a humble menial job in the world's view of things. Our forefathers on this continent had to clear the land of the wild growth of nature and win a patch of tillable soil in order to raise food for their survival. In our psychological life we do a similar thing. We clear away the wild natural growths in order to plant and nourish the impressions which will be more fruitful of health and happiness.

Thus you do not work merely to make money, to win fame, or just to keep body and soul together, but you work to realize the dignity and grandeur of yourself as a spiritual being. Keep this as your main objective along with your everyday objective and you will find that much of the burden of life falls away. Any kind of work is a burden when it is done only for money or vanity.

Here is the Master Teacher's formula for success in any field: "Let him who would be great among you be your servant." Give yourself unreservedly to any job, and that job will give back to you. It may not always give back in terms of money or worldly rewards, but if the doing of it brings you to more confidence and self-awareness, then you have gained much more than money or any worldly reward. You have gained in consciousness, and consciousness commands its rewards everywhere. Because of this you will have money and the other worldly rewards from other sources. Get to concentrating too closely upon what you are going to get out of any piece of work, and you open your mind to countless anxieties and fears and doubts and all sorts of warring thoughts and unpleasant feelings which will make your job burdensome. But if you know your true objective in life is to fulfill yourself as a person, then any old job will do, in any old place, because it will enable you to make an advance upon the worldliness of unknowing.

It is an old truism that we get out of anything exactly what we put into it, but this is not always seen by everybody in depth. Do anything constructively and with good feeling and you put the universe in your debt. It is bound to pay you back sometime, somewhere. Build a better mousetrap or a better salad bowl or a better light bulb, and as Emerson says, even if you live in the woods "the world will beat a path to your door." Alexander Graham Bell did not work for money or fame alone. He worked with a passion to transform his dream into reality. Then the money came. Every great invention or discovery is great because it has served mankind. It has freed men from toil and struggle and time and distances and provided for them a better and happier existence here on earth.

The great ones among us are those who help us to live, who save us in time of extremity or danger, who inspire us with courage and hope, who show us how the job is done. Look at the statues in the parks and public squares of any city. They are of men and women who served the rest of us, who did things for us, who advanced civilization or saved it. They were our servants, and that is why they are distinguished. We often see a picture of our President pinning a medal upon the breast of some soldier who has shown bravery on the battlefield. We the people, in whose name the President acts, will say that we are honoring this man for his bravery. Don't you believe it! We are honoring him because he saved our necks. He served us. He advanced on the darkness when and where we could not, and for this we owe and give him honor. As Robert Quillen said, "If he had been just as brave in the service of our enemy, we would teach our children to hate him." We honor those who serve us.

Do something to help people in their daily life, whether it is making a better article or giving a better service or making them happy as comedians do on the stage—serve them and they will pay you. That is why the old religious teaching is true: it is more blessed to give than to receive, for those who give of themselves get all of this world's goods and much more. They get good feeling in themselves because they have cleared the wilderness and advanced upon the darkness and made light around them.

Giving is truly the only way of getting. Beware of making a mistake here. If you give merely in order to get some reward, you will spoil the whole business. Thought of this kind steals from itself and one grows poorer. But if you give yourself to some work or service for the real goal of getting inward growth and awareness of yourself as a creative being, while envisioning and accepting material rewards also, then nothing and no one can hold the rewards away from you. This rule is stated by Jesus when he says, "Seek ye first the kingdom of heaven and its righteousness and all these other things will be added unto you." It is an everlastingly true principle, but too few have seen the way in which it is true.

All one has to give is his attitudes, his temperament, his disposition, his consciousness. Give this to any work and the results are guaranteed by universal law. Then one moves from "have to" to "want to." And he moves by divine law and under grace. A divine intelligence and not his own perfects the things that concern him. His subconscious forces, which formerly impelled and compelled him in wrong action, now harmoniously guide and conduct him in right action. This is

a great freedom, and it results in love or good feeling. Therefore it is the fulfilling of the law.

Good feeling is always characterized by wanting to instead
of having to. It is spontaneity and initiative rather than obligation and inertia. When we use the mental law correctly, the
result is good feeling, harmony, and love. A businessman who
has used this law admirably well says of his results: "My outfit
is the finest I could ever wish for. I know I make mistakes, but
do I hear about them? No! But let me do something right and
I get wires and telephone calls congratulating me. I would do
anything for this outfit." That man has drive and he has grace.
And he has money.

What I have said in these last two chapters can be summa-
rized briefly.

1. Look on every encounter as filled with good fortune.

2. Recognize that you are one with God and therefore the
Presence of Mind which knows all things is where you are.

3. Do your job with good feeling, but expect your rewards
from God or Life.

4. In any adversity, stop thinking of what the situation is
doing to you and think of what you are doing to the situation
with your attitude.

5. Don't trust your goodness; trust your consciousness.

6. Keep marshaling your principles and keep your mental
tools in good order.

7. Pray much in good times, and you will be all prayed up
for bad times.

8. Use your inferiority as a mainspring.

9. Don't complain about your job. Any job is the best job
in the world.

10. Be a good servant, and the world will pay you and make
you boss.

Teach Me to Die

"It is not death," said Montaigne, "it is dying that alarms me." There are few of us whom it does not alarm. It has been called the last enemy. But since death is an inevitable part of life, not death itself but the fear of death should be the last enemy to be overcome. Indeed, fear is the only enemy of our life here—the fear of want, of injury, of illness, of loss, and a thousand anonymous fears that dog us in the wilderness of uncertainty and knowing. I have dealt with many of these fears above, and now we come to this greatest of evils—or, perhaps, the greatest good. If death is a friend, we ought to prepare to entertain him; if an enemy, to overcome him. Certainly death can be formidable and fearful only when he comes as a stranger.

Once, as I sat beside a woman who was dying, she looked at me and said, "you taught me how to live, now teach me how to die." But because she had learned how to live, she already knew how to die. I covet the next little space on this paper, and the reader's indulgence, to memorialize my friend Gus. Gus was a dachshund who lived nobly and died the same. Often, when I sat at my desk and he was in his basket nearby, our eyes would meet and I would say, in Bible words, "O

King, live forever—but when you go, go nobly, as you have lived." He did. Old and full of years, without a struggle, he slept, and, as I believe, waked beyond my awareness. In many ways, animals are more noble in their living and dying than men. An old cat, apparently healthy and happy, asked his master to let him out one morning. He stood for a few seconds on the threshhold blinking in the sunshine and twitching his magnificent tail. Then he walked to a large flat rock in the sun, curled up his body and left it as an unneeded garment.

It takes good living to die nobly, and I use the word good as I have throughout these pages, as meaning not moralistically good but enlightened. When we begin our lives, death is far away and unreal. It happens to others, never in our family. Sad indeed is the plight of those to whom death comes as a stranger. If they have not at times before called up the Unthinkable and made their peace with it, they are overwhelmed. They are even angry that it should happen to them, that their loved one be taken away in so peremptory a manner. They resent the injustice of it all. Never was grief like theirs. They have to learn two lessons at once—how and what to think of death, and how to bear grief. Every emotion is part of life's symphony; it is how we put the moods together that determines music or dissonance. True grief is noble and ought to be nobly experienced and expressed and conquered. Grief is cleansing, humanizing, and strengthening. It hallows the heart.

But grief prolonged is selfish. It means we are thinking more of our own loss than the departed one's gain. At least when one dies after much suffering, death is a release, and if the philosophy and religion of five thousand years and the instincts of the human heart are right in suggesting the continuity of life beyond the grave, then part of us at least can rejoice that "death hath set him free." If death ends all, and there is nothing hereafter, there is still relief from pain and suffering and the thralldom of the flesh.

But since the beginning of history the vast plurality of mankind have believed in some kind of existence after death. Horace, the Roman poet, in Ode No. 30 in the third book put it particularly well (the English rendering is by E. B. W. Chappelow).

> Not all of me will die, not all of me
> Pass hence to unrelieved oblivion;
> Some quintessential spark must needs break free
> And soar and seek and touch at last the sun.
> Else were the very breath of life a liar,
> Which hath thereof, since my first sentient hour,
> Instinctive been a certitude, a star,
> a motive unto action, and a power.
> How otherwise could viewless poesy
> Prick me to render things invisible
> Half glimpsed through magic phrases, how and why
> Urge me unresting, bind me with a spell even,
> To echo forth, tho' faint, scarce audible,
> The ultimate music of the heart of heaven?*

When his followers asked him how they should bury his body, Socrates replied, "You cannot bury Socrates. You can bury my body, but you can't put me in a grave." The words of Horace and Socrates and thousands like them inspire us and give us hope, but they do not prove anything conclusively. Probably the most significant announcement ever made about this subject—significant because it contains both faith and science—is in the declaration of Jesus: "I am the resurrection and the life: he that believeth in me, though he were dead, yet shall he live and whosoever liveth and believeth in me shall never die" (John 11). Martha, whose brother Lazarus was dead, had just been affirming her faith that he would rise again in the resurrection at the last day. In common with most of mankind, she lived in hope that sometime, somewhere, somehow her brother would live again.

Some have even interpreted the resurrection to mean that

---

*Horace, *Odes*, E. B. W. Chappelow, trans. (*The London Spectator*; quoted in *The Literary Digest*, ca. 1930).

after a time in the grave the physical body would rise again. But Jesus' reply to her is arresting and jolting. He affirms the resurrection as a present state and not one to be arrived at in process of time. Here is something to wrestle with. Perhaps death is in us who say we are living and not in those we call dead. Perhaps too, *I AM-ness* encompasses and includes both life and death without diminishment or hurt. How this might be we shall see a little further on. For the present, let us stay a while longer with the hope and instinct of the ages that "not all of me will die," and the question of how to face the test when it comes.

Anyone who has watched and listened with the dying knows that they often see something that cheers them on. Edison, in his chair, would lapse into a coma and then open his eyes and smile and say, "It is very beautiful over there." My brother, at twenty-eight, would rouse and say to another brother, "There is power there." And another in his last moments whispered, "I wish I had the power of writing or speaking, for then I would describe to you how pleasant a thing it is to die." All these instincts and hopes and intimations have sustained generations from the ancient Egyptian to the modern astronaut. But hope is first cousin to fear, and without something more substantial the human heart still has its sorrow and its loneliness.

It is helpful to remember that these too have their good offices—that our grief comes to make us stronger to conquer the small troubles and to understand our kind. It is helpful to remember that anything so universal as death cannot be all bad. We who suffer because another has departed have not been singled out by Fate for some special burden.

That skillful writer Leo Rosten, in one of his *"Five Stories from Five Faiths,"* tells of the Eastern woman who, having lost her firstborn, was so beset by grief that she wandered through the streets pleading for some magic medicine to restore the life of her child. She was told that there was one who could help her, the Perfect One who lived at the top of the mountain: "Go to him and ask." She did, and the Perfect One told her to go back into the city from house to house and "bring to me a mustard seed from a house in which no one has ever, died." You know the sequel. She could find no such house. The inevitable and freeing conclusion formed in her mind: she was not the only one who had suffered at the hands of death. What is so universal must have some element of Providence.

In *Erewhon and Erewhon Revisited* Samuel Butler says of the unborn,

They have no knowledge and cannot even conceive of the existence of anything that is not such as they are themselves. Those who have been born are to them what the dead are to us. They can see no light in them and know no more about them than they do of any stage in their own past development other than the ones through which they are passing at the moment. They do not even know that their mothers are alive—much less that their mothers were once as they are now. To an embryo, its mother is simply the environment and is looked upon much as our inorganic surroundings are by themselves.

The great terror of their lives is the fear of birth—that they shall have to leave the only thing that they can think of as life and enter upon a darkened unknown which to them is tantamount to annihilation.

Some, indeed, among them have maintained that birth is not the death which they commonly deem it, but that there is life beyond the womb of which they as yet know nothing and which is a million-fold more truly life than anything they have yet been able even to imagine. But the greater number shake their yet unfashioned heads and say they have no evidence for this that will stand a moment's examination. "Nay," answer the others, "so much work, so elaborate, so wondrous is that whereon we are now so busily engaged must have a purpose though the purpose is beyond our grasp." "Never!" reply the first speakers: "Our pleasure in the work is sufficient justification for it. Who has ever partaken of this life you speak of, and re-entered into the womb to tell us of it? Granted that some few have pretended to have done this, but how completely have their stories broken down when subjected to the tests of sober criticism. No. When we are born, we are born and there is an end of us."

But in the hour of birth, when they can no longer re-enter the womb and tell the others, Behold! they find it is not so.

Reasoning like this is helpful after the first hours or days or weeks of grieving are over. In the beginning, grief is too poignant for one who is unprepared to meet the stranger. The thing to do then is to remember, as Evelyn Ardis Whitman once reminded us, that you are sick now and this is the period of convalescence. Your whole spiritual-physical system has suffered a great shock and you must rest, sleep, eat, and stay out in the open as much as possible. You must treat yourself as you really are, a patient who is convalescing from sickness. The reason we call one who is sick and being treated a patient is because patience is the way back to health. So many people in their sufferings and misfortunes grow angry and reproachful. This is the wrong way to get strong or well. Give yourself time and quiet to recover and every day you will be a little better, and with patience you will be able to live again and, as one wife suggested in a note to her husband before she died, "For my sake turn to life again. Complete the dear unfinished tasks of mine, and therein perchance I may comfort you."

The noblest, most royal and admirable reaction I ever heard from a grieving heart came from the widow of a physician. We had just buried her husband's body, and as we rode home in the car she said to me, "I thank God that I can bear this grief for him." Later, in that splendid volume *The Search for Meaning* by Victor Frankel, M.D., I found another shining example of how grief may be turned to the account of life. An aged friend and fellow physician, recently widowed, seemed unable to live with his burden of grief. He had sought the counsel and direction of others but was still inconsolable. At last he came to his friend and colleague. Dr. Frankel asked him, "How would it be if you had died first?" "Oh," he replied, "she could not have borne it." "Then be thankful," suggested Dr. Frankel, "that you have the opportunity of bearing this burden for her." Without a word more the old man rose, thanked his friend, and departed, satisfied. He had a reason now for lifting up his head and brightening his eye and quickening his step. He could use his grief constructively. He could give it as a gift to his beloved. There is always healing in giving. We are always at our best when giving ourselves to others. Every experience and quality in life, whether it be termed good or bad, is useful for some purpose. Even grief can be turned to account and made a part of life. Dr. Frankel found out in the prison camp of Auschwitz the truth of Nietzsche's statement, "A man can stand almost any how if he has a why."

Anyone who has ever lost a loved one knows the darkness and emptiness of those first hours. Anyone who has stood staring into an open grave knows the utter devastation of the spirit and the doubt that life will ever be good again. It is difficult to sleep, and if you sleep at all you may dream of your loved one only to waken to the cruel reality. You try not to remember, and yet when you have had a brief spell of blessed forgetfulness you reproach yourself for having forgotten. You remember all the little things you would like to say to the loved one, which cannot be said now, and all the countless things you ought to have done or might have done, and you bitterly accuse yourself of your own faults and failures and neglect. It is a common, almost universal reaction. Nearly every grief-stricken person tortures himself somewhat with the thought of what he might have done more.

Your friends and all who love you try to help, but they cannot reach you. If ever words fail, they fail now. You are lost, lonely, and desolate. Every attempt to divert you only makes the pain the sharper. The thing for this is to remember that you are sick and you are a patient, and patience is the way back. There is a gap in your psyche. It is like a lesion in the flesh, but it will heal. Those are not idle words which say of marriage that "the twain shall be one flesh." They are one flesh in the form of their children, of course. But there is another way in which they are one. People who live together grow together psychically. There is a psychic fusion. Husbands and wives know what the other person is thinking or how he or she is feeling. When this bond is broken at death there is a wound, and it bleeds. Like the wound of Amfortas, no outward ministration can help it; healing comes only through spiritual renewal. Those who know this are more prepared to meet the stranger.

I recall an old friend of mine and the time when I was a young apprentice minister. I conducted a funeral service for one of her sisters. Afterward, we went to the home. There, over Swedish cookies and strong Swedish coffee, she showed me how to banish selfish grief. Alma Nelson had been born in Sweden with a left arm that extended no farther than the elbow joint. She was near seventy at the time I speak of, had never been married but had raised two families, her dead brother's and her sister's. She was as stalwart a soul as ever I had known, and her grief was too dignified and meaningful to indulge in self-reproach, self-pity, or resentment of life. She said, "Sister is free. I know that and I am glad for her." When her many friends came calling, she met them at the door and said, kindly but firmly, "If you have come to weep with me please go back but if you have come to strengthen me, please come in."

Our literature is full of illustrations, parables, and analogies, all devised to help us face the problem of loss by death. Here is one. The heart that suffers will find something in it. Once a man rode on a certain train of whose destination he knew nothing. But there was good companionship among the passengers. There was laughter and there were talk and music and plans made together for the days ahead. It was a good life except that now and then a loved fellow passenger would leave the train without warning. The man wept over the going of his friend. "It is not fair," he said. "If we could only know where they are and what they are doing." Then one day a light tap fell on his shoulder and in the swiftness of a moment, he was outside on the station platform and the train was roaring on without him. All around were familiar faces, friends of long ago who had come to greet him and welcome him. On every side was light and beauty and peace incomparably more lovely, more precious than the stuffy limits of the train. The man turned reproachfully to the Presence beside him. "Why could we not have known?" he cried. "Why weren't we told it would be like this?"

"My son," said the grave and gentle voice, "if you had known your destination and the littleness of your journey, would you have troubled with good friends and good music on the way?"

That little parable is someone's earnest effort to express what he felt or believed, or wanted to believe, or at least wanted others to believe about this experience in life called death. It has the merit of illustrating that there is meaning in our existence; that everything we think and everything we do and every action and response to life is meaningful and leads to some good end, what and where we do not know. Hope and instinct tell us it is good and right and beautiful, but if we knew that we were going there by some predestined fate, we would not heed the meaning of the present hour or realize that the only life we have is the life of the moment, and so we would not develop an understanding and appreciation of the end, however grand. The only real life we know is this little spot of light between birth and death. That much is certain. Get the most out of it every day and every hour and you have that much in the bank. They can't take that away from you. If you find meaning in the hour, you can trust the larger meaning that ordained that meaning.

Thus far in this chapter I have spoken speculatively about death. We have been reasoning analogically and considering practical responses and reactions. From ancient times this has been the standard way of thinking about and reacting to death—to find analogies in nature to help bolster our faith that life goes on. As a writer of the last century (Alger) says,

Man, holding his conscious being precious beyond all things, and shrinking with pervasive anxieties from the moment of destined dissolution, looks around through the realms of nature, with thoughtful eye, in search of parallel phenomena further developed, significant sequels in other creatures' fates, whose evolution and fulfillment may happily throw light on his own. . . . Seeing the snake cast its old slough and glide forth renewed, he can see so in death man but sheds his fleshly exuviae, while the spirit emerges, regenerate. He beholds the beetle break from its filthy sepulchre and commence its summer work; and straightway he hangs a golden scarabaeus in his temples as an emblem of a future life. After vegetations' wintry deaths, hailing the returning spring that brings resurrection and life to the graves of the sod, he dreams of some far-off spring of humanity, yet to come, when the frosts of man's untoward doom shall relent and all the costly seeds sown through ages in the great-earth-tomb shall shoot up in celestial shapes . . . having watched the silkworm, as it wove its cocoon and lay down in its oblong grave apparently dead, until at length it struggles forth, glittering with rainbow colors a winged moth, endowed with new faculties and living a new life in a new sphere, he conceives that so the human soul may, in the fullness of time, disentangle itself from the imprisoning meshes of this world of larvae, a thing of spirit beauty, to sail through heavenly airs; and henceforth he engraves a butterfly on the tombstone in vivid prophecy of immortality. Thus a moralising observation of natural similitudes teaches man to hope for an existence beyond death.*

But similitudes and analogies in nature, though suggestive and inspiring, leave us still uncertain. Man wants something, needs something more. If a thing is true, there is a way in which it is true and it is that way that we want. Has modern science, which has rescued so much of our life from ignorance and misconception and superstition, nothing to say about this important concern? It has. And that is what we are on the track

*Quoted by Thompson J. Hudson in *A Scientific Demonstration of the Future Life* (Chicago: A. C. McClurg & Co., 1909), 10th ed., p. 35.

of in the final portions of this chapter. There has existed for more than a hundred years, roughly corresponding with the age of modern science, a field of observation and investigation which affords at least presumptive evidence of immortality. I refer to the phenomena of mesmerism, hypnotism, spiritualism, and all subjective activity and psychic phenomena. For a comprehensive study of this field of scientific investigation, I refer the reader to an unusual book which has only recently been reprinted, *The Law Of Psychic Phenomena* by Thompson J. Hudson.* Until the first publication of this volume in 1892, no one had ever applied the methods of inductive science to psychological phenomena. Up until that time men had philosophized about man as composed of "body, soul, and spirit" or "body, mind, and spirit." But what they meant by these terms was never quite clear. Sometimes soul and spirit were synonymous, sometimes they were different. The same confusion attaches to the word mind throughout all literature. As we have seen earlier, the most workable definition for mind is that it is "a medium for impressions." The great discovery of the nineteenth century was that man has two minds, or if you prefer, two levels of one mind: the conscious mind with its five senses and inductive reasoning powers, and the subconscious mind, which is a memory bank of all consciously perceived impressions and the governor of all the automatic motions and fuctions of the body, such as heartbeat, digestion, and assimilation. Hudson called these two the objective and the subjective minds and marshaled from all the phenomena previously mentioned the data and evidence of the particular and peculiar functions of these two minds.

Up until this time there existed great confusion (and still does in the minds of those who do not know the facts) as to how a person could survive bodily death, since the mind was connected with the brain. The brain dies with the body. If you were to ask any knowledgeable person what in his view would

---

*New York: Samuel Weiser, 1968.

constitute conclusive evidence of continuity of life in man, he would probably reply that he must first be convinced that the mind does not follow the conditions of the body and the brain. Some would remind us that all human experience goes to show that as the body grows weaker, the mind grows weaker; that a disease of the brain produces insanity or imbecility; that certain organs of the mind can be modified, inhibited, or totally destroyed by chemicals or a surgical operation; that mechanical pressure upon the brain produces total unconsciousness and insensibility; that when the body dies, all manifestations of mind cease at once and forever.

All of this is true so far as the objective mind is concerned, but it has been demonstrated that man has a dual mind, two planes of consciousness—a normal and a superplane—and that the latter manifests itself when the former is inhibited. In other words, when the brain is asleep and all the objective senses and faculties are in complete abeyance, the supernormal or subjective faculties are capable of intense activity, as is to be seen in the phenomena of hypnotism and spiritualism and trance-speaking and many similar phenomena. The objective mind is merely the function of the human brain and necessarily ceases with the death of the body; whereas the subjective mind belongs to a distinct entity, which is apparently capable of sustaining an existence independently of the body. It is this entity that has been called the soul in man.

What is it that the average person would consider essential in a life to come? Clearly it would be the retention of conscious individuality. Whether the soul of man retains its identity after the death of the body is second only in interest and importance to the question of immortality. There are many who have held and still hold that the soul is necessarily reabsorbed into the universal as "the dewdrop drops into the shining sea." But this presupposes the loss of identity, which to most of us would be considered tantamount to annihilation. However, Hudson says, "There is abundant evidence in phenomena observable in this life to demonstrate, as far as such a proposition is demonstrable, that the soul does retain its identity in a more pronounced degree, if possible, than we can retain it in this objective existence." In what does identity exist or how is it retained? The answer is obviously through consciousness and memory. If either is lost, identity is lost.

Let us recapitulate some of the demonstrable facts which Hudson first brought together. One of the most significant discoveries and demonstrations is that, as the power of the objective mind weakens, the power of the subjective mind increases dramatically. The subjective operates independently of the brain and the conscious mind. It perceives by intuition and communicates by telepathy or what today is called extra-sensory perception. It is the storehouse of memory. It performs its highest function when the objective senses are in abeyance. It is apparently capable of sustaining an existence independently of brain and body.

The objective mind is a mind of inquiry. It reasons inductively, that is, by collecting and classifying facts in order to arrive at an understanding of a general principle or law. The subjective mind reasons only deductively. That is, it will take any premise or suggestion and with uncanny accuracy marshal all the facts in support of that idea and persistently ignore all facts that militate against it. The subjective mind will not argue or engage in controversy. It is dogmatic and absolute. The subjective is the seat of the instinct toward self-preservation and is concerned with the defense and protection of the organism. When disease causes the body to weaken, the objective mind grows correspondingly weak. Not so the subjective. As the body becomes weak, the subjective mind grows stronger, and is strongest in the hour of death. When death approaches and its inevitability is realized, it is no longer feared, and pain ceases. At that supreme moment the subjective mind takes complete possession and the objective senses are benumbed, the body is anaesthetized, and the patient dies "without pain and without regret."

At the supreme moment his soul is in active communion with loved ones at a distance, and the death message is often, when psychic conditions are favorable, consciously received. The records of telepathy demonstrate this proposition. Nay, more; they may be cited to show that in the hour of death the soul is capable of projecting a fantasm of such strength and objectivity that it may be an object of sensorial experience to those for whom it is intended. Moreover, it has happened that telepathic messages have been sent by the dying, at the moment of dissolution, giving all the particulars of the tragedy, when the death was caused by an unexpected blow which crushed the skull of a victim. It is obvious that in such a case it is impossible that the objective mind could have participated in the transaction. The evidence is, indeed, overwhelming, that, no matter what form death may assume, whether caused by lingering disease, old age, or violence, the subjective mind is never weakened by its approach or its presence. On the other hand, that the objective mind weakens with the body and perishes with the brain, is a fact confirmed by every-day observation and universal experience.*

A sober reflection on these arresting facts and the details concerning them, all demonstrable by experiment, forces us to conclude that here in man is the seat of the soul, possession of God-like qualities and capacities, independent of brain and body, perfect in knowledge and memory, transcendent of all harm or hurt—it is Emmanuel or "God with us." It is the Christ of whom Paul said (1 Cor. 15), "If Christ be not risen, then is our preaching vain and your faith is also vain." But one who studies these truths of being will readily perceive that Christ was dead only when consciousness was objective and subjective consciousness was submerged. And Christ rises whenever a person is made aware of his transcendental equipment and being.

This state is the *other life* to which we all are tending, and which religion speaks of as *the hereafter*. We enter this *other life* not as a consequence of somatic death but as the result of increased awareness or, as religion puts it, "being born

*Thompson J. Hudson, *A Scientific Demonstration of the Future Life,* pp. 223–24.

again." This *other life* is not in time but in us now. It is the Infinite and Original life, and we are alive with it now even though for the most part we are generally unaware. The life we are now living is the life of God and it is eternal. When we do not know it, we project it into the future. When the eyes are opened and the ears are unstopped, then consciousness is born again, we rise from the dead, and original sin (the submersion of spiritual faculties) is forgiven or eradicated.

One often reads the prophecy of Steinmetz, the electrical genius of Schenectady, that in the next fifty years the great discoveries will be made in the field of investigation of the spiritual nature and faculties and powers of man. Perhaps it will take another fifty years, but sometime the inductive methods of science will be turned upon this field of investigation. Then religion may emerge from the realm of mythology, superstition, dogma, and blind faith, for as Einstein observed, "Science without religion is lame, religion without science is blind."*

Then every man will be able to "give a reason for the faith that is in him."

*Albert Einstein, *Out of My Later Years* (Westport, Conn.: Greenwood Press, Inc., 1950), p. 26.

Let It Be

Let it be! These are indeed words of wisdom, release, and freedom. There are so many things to vex, and only one to soothe. We have seen that we suffer from our opinions and our judgments and not from facts and things. Therefore withhold judgment and let your opinion lie still, and you will have no hurt. There are many ways of saying this. Willard and Marguerite Beecher say, "Let go and walk on." Our proverbs say: Let sleeping dogs lie, and Don't cry over spilt milk. Satchel Leroy Paige advises, "Don't look back, something may be gaining on you." However you say it, it is a practical and useful tool in thinking and living.

In this book I have tried to furnish tools and handles by which you can manage your psychology and then let your psychology handle your affairs. That is our business. Let us attend to business confident that a man who is diligent in his business "shall stand before kings." I have tried to put things in perspective, pointing out what is primarily important and relatively unimportant: thoughts always, things never. When Socrates was dying, he told his heavy-hearted friends, "I bid you think of Truth and not of Socrates." That is the perennial formula for getting out of trouble or removing hurt feelings, for assuaging anxiety and worry and for every one of life's difficulties. The mind magnifies what it looks upon and deals with. To withdraw the mind will reduce the size of the problem. But magnetized to the problem, the mind cannot withdraw unless it has another pole to turn to. Truth is that pole. When troubled or vexed, turn to the highest truth you know and let it capture your attention and polarize your thought. In obedience to truth, the mind will let the trouble go.

The technique of letting go of the wrong handles and taking hold of the right ones is often difficult to learn. A mother is bitter and resentful. Her daughter of eighteen years has left home in order to get away from the mother's overbearing ways. The girl has left college temporarily, found a job, taken a dismal apartment, and for a while slept on the floor, having no furniture. Soon she meets a young man and they marry. Now the mother feels betrayed and lost because her life has been centered around the child. Life is teaching her to let go. Her burden is her thought. She has no other. The Emperor says, "When you happen to be ruffled a little by any untoward accident, retire immediately into your reason and do not move out of tune any further than needs must. For the sooner you return to harmony, the more you will get the situation in your own power."* Vexing situations keep repeating themselves in the life of one who has not found his inner harmony. When that is achieved, then—as we have seen earlier—"against Israel shall not a dog lift his tongue."

A man of thirty-five said: "My mother is a dear, but she irritates me no end. If I'm out late or ask a friend to dinner I have to pay for it. For the next two or three days she is helpless with asthma!" Possessive parents are an old story. For them healing and happiness come only when they "let go and let God." Or, as the Psalmist points out, "The sacrifices of God are a broken spirit; a broken and contrite heart" (Ps. 51).

A broken spirit or a broken heart means a changed feeling.

*Marcus Aurelius, *Meditations,* Jeremy Collier, trans. (London: Walter Scott, Ltd.), Bk. 6, par. 11.

Leave your indignation and walk on in inward peace. You are not a judge but a beholder. Learn to love unselfishly. Hold the one or the thing that you love as though it were a beautiful bird in the palm of your hand. Acknowledge its perfect freedom to do exactly what it wants to do: to leave or to stay. Be grateful that it was willing to live with you for a time. Be willing for it to leave at any time. Grant it its freedom. If you love like that, you will hold but not possess, for no one wants to flee from a love like that.

But love selfishly, and you crush the bird in the closed hand. We all know people who get sick when they cannot control others. We all know people who hold a club over other members of the family by saying, "You'll be sorry when I am gone" or "My heart is not going to last much longer." They threaten you with a heart attack in the next twenty-four hours if you do not do exactly what they want you to do. This is nothing but selfishness and overpossessiveness. Such a heart needs to be broken apart, psychologically speaking, its poorer part left behind and its better part carried forward into life.

I know a woman who was married to a surgeon after World War I. The doctor had returned from the war gassed and an invalid and selfishly possessive of his beautiful wife. She loved him and nursed him, but he was always threatening to kill himself and frequently tried to do so. Periodically, he would go to the bathroom and slit his wrists. Then the distracted, nervous wife, almost frightened out of her skin, would bind his wounds and nurse him back to health. If the cuts were deep, she would get the family doctor to suture them, and all would be well again for a while. But she never knew at what hour of day or night this might happen again. The husband held this psychological control over his wife for years, until finally she took up the teaching of modern metaphysics. She learned that what he was doing was bad for him and for her. She knew that neither would be free until both were free, and that she had to be the one who would walk away from this bondage. She knew she had to be the strong one, that she would have to let him go and walk on in her heart. Only in this way could she release him to his larger freedom.

On a certain evening he again threatened to kill himself, but the wife had decided that she would never again give in to this blackmail and that, living or dying, he must grow. She went to bed quaking beneath the covers. She heard him go to the bathroom. She knew quite well what he was about to do. But she had determined not to move from that bed. The usual thing happened, and a neighbor heard the commotion, came in, and saved him. The wife had never stirred from her bed. Her act had immediate impact upon her husband, and he never attempted suicide again. The false control he had over her was broken. Their love was on a freer, more natural basis. She had let go of the lesser and polarized her thought with the greater.

People often suffer from the value judgments of other people. They cannot feel right unless somebody praises or approves of them. They are dependent upon this approval from other people, and cast down when they feel that praise is owed but denied them. They are lifted up under the smile of others. But theirs is a position of weakness wholly dependent upon what others do or do not do. We all need the esteem of our fellows, yet we ought not to be dependent upon it. As the old saying has it, "Applause is the spur of noble minds, the end and aim of weak ones." The frown of others is painful to one who expects approval—like the account of the comedian's dream. He was before a vast audience telling jokes and singing songs, but something was wrong: nobody applauded. "That's hell for a comedian." But this problem, again, is due to failure to put first things first. Fate can never rob you of deserved applause. Find your inner center, thrill to your divine prerogatives, hold fast to these and walk on, letting all else go. Jefferson observed in a letter to a friend, "Go on deserving applause and you will be sure to meet with it."

We have all met what I. A. R. Wylie called "the grievance collector." Miss Wylie described a woman who lived next

door. A low wall divided their back yards. Over this wall the
two women occasionally exchanged greetings and advice. Every comment Miss Wylie made was met with some bitter,
common nagging complaint. Either there was too much sun,
or the single tree in the Wylie yard was throwing too much
shade on the other yard, or the woman had been sold inferior
bulbs, or children and dogs were trampling her flowerbeds.
Out of patience one day with all this, Miss Wylie said to her,
"If you ever admitted that anything went right with you, I
should fall in a dead faint." The neighbor never spoke to her
again. She had been deprived of her one great satisfaction in
life—her grievance against it. She suffered from her opinion.

There is something in each of us that wants to enjoy a good
wrong. If it is indulged, we can easily fall into the habit of
being a grievance collector. Such people collect grievances not
only against other people but against life itself, against God
and the universe. They say, "If God is love, why doesn't he
cure the evil in the world? Why does he allow pain? Why did
he not make us without the tendency to think and to do evil?
Why does he allow the appalling injustices and sorrow?" They
forget that the God they are talking about is not individual but
universal. The Universal does not, because it cannot, deal with
individual details. All of its works are finished. It has placed
its nature in us, and that is the God who does things and makes
things.

Judge Troward has pointed out (*The Edinburgh Lectures*) that
the Universal cannot act on the plane of the particular without
itself becoming the particular. Being is one, but it has two
poles, the Universal and the individual or particular. Being is
like a stick. It has two ends. One end is the Universal or God;
the other is the individual or man. They are one, but their
spheres of operation are different in degree. God cannot cure
the hurts of the world without the agency of man, who is the
other pole of the single being.

If you are angry because others misbehave, are unjust, or
have bad breath, what will you do to relieve your anger and

cure your hurt? You can talk to them, advise and teach, and if they are responsive they may change and all is well. But if they do not change, will you go on hurting because of your judgment? Or will you reflect that each person does what he is compelled to do by his inner nature? He can do no other. Then cease your censure and walk on. Perhaps your example will be a better teacher. If your light shines before men and they see your good works, they may glorify the source of them, your Father in heaven.

The world is full of cruel and rude and ugly people, people who hurt inside for some reason or other and therefore unconsciously want to make others hurt. We meet them everywhere. Why are we hurt by them? It is because of our expectation. If we did not expect them to act otherwise, we should not be hurt when they behave as they do. A friend of mine was about to park in a certain place in a parking lot. But in the next space a car was parked at the wrong angle and the driver was sitting in it. My friend said, "I thought as I tried to move in he would understand my predicament, and being a gentlemen, would move his car a few feet and let me in." But the driver of that car was not a gentleman, and he only glared at my friend, who got out of his car and went over to the man and asked him politely if he would move a little. The answer was a gruff "No!" Then my friend hunted out the parking-lot attendant and asked him if he would make the man move. The attendant hemmed and hawed a bit and finally agreed that the uniformed guard who had a gun had more authority than he. The guard came and spoke to the man, who still refused to move an inch, saying, "I'm staying right here."

Now, my friend who wanted this parking place thought to appeal to the city policeman, since the parking policeman had no effect on the recalcitrant man in the car. But the city policeman said he had no authority to move the man either, since this was a private parking lot. The stubborn character in the car apparently knew this all the while and was morbidly exulting in his little hour of dominance.

Well, here you have Aesop's old story of the dog in the manger. The man could not use two parking places; he could only use one, but he was not going to let anybody else use the other. His action had something to do with what was going on inside of him and with his general attitude toward people and life. This kind of character is abroad in the world. He was here when Akhenaton and Nefertiti brought enlightenment to Egypt. He was here with Socrates and Jesus. No doubt he will be here many generations hence. Let us be realists and accept this fact unless and until we can change it. Let us go a step further and realize that our success and happiness do not depend for an instant upon the conduct of characters like this, but rather entirely upon our inward measure of strength and harmony. This man's action may thwart our present endeavor to park, but that is quite a temporary thing. Leave him to heaven and walk on. After all, if it gives you some small comfort to know, heaven is dealing with him already. A man's rewards and punishments are from his own nature. He is what he is and I am what I am and you are what you are, and only these realities determine our progress and our happiness. So my friend kept his composure and looked for another parking place and found it. He let go and walked—or rather drove—on.

We have to learn to walk away from many things, to let them drop from us. A person who is brought up feeling hurt, unloved, and unpopular develops an emotional goal of humiliation and defeat and failure. Failure is the thing he is accustomed to, being hurt and hurting is what he loves; it is his only emotional excitement. Harmony and right order are foreign lands to him.

Many a person thinks he wants to be happy, but will discover that he actually wants to be sad. He has an emotional accent of sadness and humiliation, and this is compelling him toward goals of sadness and humiliation. There are people who have the emotional goal of finding nothing in this life of satisfaction. They feel that nothing will turn out right; everything is bound to fail. They say, "For me it never happens right." For them the counsel of William James is in order: "Action and feeling go together. There's no more useful precept than that which bids us pay primary attention to what we do and express and not care too much for what we feel."*

Don't wrestle with the bad feeling, don't fight the problem; do and act the best you know in spite of how you feel, and return to your center of inward sovereignty and walk on. "Agree with thine adversary quickly, whilst thou art in the way with him; lest at any time the adversary deliver thee to the judge, and the judge deliver thee to the officer and thou be cast into prison" (Matt. 5). If you are in a dispute with another person, does this mean that you should let him have his way? By no means. It simply means that you should come to terms. Disputation and all troublesome emotion indicate a circular movement within. One is not going anywhere. In order to go straight again, one must come to terms with his own emotional turmoil.

The way to do this is to remember that the adversary is never a person or a situation but rather our thought about these. If we think that we have been hurt, diminished, or deprived, or if we think that we are threatened or can be robbed or diminished, then it is our thought that we have to revise. Recall that it is attitudes and not circumstances that determine our progress. At this point one ought to be able to envision himself as moving forward in spite of the presently troublesome situation. Thus the thing to do is to come quickly to this realization and inward agreement lest, if it continue, one make the mistake of considering the circumstances as the problem, and engender fear and anger and indignation and a host of bad feelings. Then you are delivered to the judge, which means that you form a judgment and settle down in the emotional welter of your own judgment. A judgment is a settled opinion and a fixed view of things. This fixed opinion

---

* *Talks to Teachers* (New York: Henry Holt & Co., 1902), pp. 200–201.

will put you in prison and confirm you in the problem. The more you struggle to get out, the stronger the prison becomes. How quickly emancipating it is simply to return to your principle and to think: all is opinion; this situation can be neither more nor less to me than I make of it. What is in control here —events or my opinion? Do you see what instant magic there is in withholding your judgment and stopping your opinion? Presto, you are free! You are out of your emotional jail, and all your involuntary forces are proceeding on the path of life and progress. That is to say, the God in you is at work in place of the argumentative intellect. You have let go and let God. This is the indirect action of the soul and it often succeeds when direct action of the mind fails.

There is another area where the attitude of Let It Be works wonders. Most of us are at some time thrown into a troublesome vortex of events and conditions we did not consciously choose. Oftentimes there is no discernible way out. There is nothing one can do outwardly and directly about the events that presently confront him. The first step in healing and renewal is to admit that the events have happened and not to argue with the fact, lest you arouse tension and frustration and anger and thereby close the doors of refreshment. As the old proverb puts it, "You cannot saw sawdust." You cannot go around and around mentally with your problem and beg the question and cry over spilt milk or wish for the water that has already gone over the dam or under the bridge—you cannot do this and come to quick solutions.

The event has happened. Be willing to have it so. There are an awful lot of folk who resent the event after it has happened, and that means they are keeping it alive. To resent means "to feel again." That is what hate does: it feels again and again and again. That is what anger does: it goes over and over the situation and wraps it in bad feeling. It won't let a matter go. Something has happened. Feel as you will about it but don't go on refeeling it, else you "bear sin for another" (Lev. 19:-17). To "Suffer sin upon thy neighbor," as Moses puts it, is to allow wrong feeling to go on in yourself because of what your neighbor has done or not done, has said or not said.

So you can relive a situation and keep it alive forever, vivified with your thought, or you can let your opinion lie still and let all bad feeling ooze away. It is the tendency of many to condemn themselves unmercifully for mistakes and failures. But Paul advises, "Happy is he that condemneth not himself in that thing which he alloweth" (Rom. 14:22). It has happened! Let it be! So you made a mistake, you failed, you came short of your goal, you are chagrined, put out, embarassed, or cast down. Beware of resenting any of those facts. There is an immediate release of tension when one admits that we all make mistakes and fail. But one should quickly match this admission with the knowledge that failure is not defeat. Our failures only indicate that we are trying for new summits of achievement, and if we are not failing we are not trying. It is not the individual failure that matters, but rather the overall progress. As the Chinese put it, "The fault is not in falling down, it is in lying there." There are none so tense as those who try to be outwardly perfect. There is great release in acknowledging your foibles and laughing at your mistakes. Man is spiritually perfect, and to acknowledge and reflect upon that Truth is constantly to improve the outer man who makes mistakes. But to claim perfection for the outer man on the basis of the spiritual truth is to confuse the intellect and plunge the emotions into a welter of tension and torment. Think of truth but not of Socrates, and you will maintain equanimity and peace and power. "Great peace have they who love thy law and nothing shall offend them." Not even their failures and mistakes!

A Zen story tells of the old Chinese walking through a crowded market place with a stick over his shoulder and on the end of the stick a jar of soup. The crowd jostled him, and the jug fell and broke and the contents spilled. Someone ran after him and said, "Your jug has fallen and broken and your soup is spilled." The informer was more excited than the old gentleman. He, with all his Oriental calm, walked straight on and said, "I know; I heard it fall!" To be willing to have it so means that you simply acknowledge that the event has happened; the event cannot be changed. It is useless to argue over it and cry out against the injustice of it all. That only produces more tension and gets one locked in or hung up on failure. After all, you still have the most precious of all goods, your knowledge of the Law, and with that you can make more soup or buy it and go from strength to strength and from glory to glory. Emulate Brother Lawrence who, when he broke a dish or made any mistake, confided to his God: "I will never do anything else unless Thou help me."

Attend not to the broken jar (clean up the mess, of course), but attend to yourself and build yourself up and think of yourself as a spiritual being, enfranchised by heaven, by nature, governed by God, and that your promotion is always from the spirit. Single events or a series of events on earth are not arbiters of destiny, and if your spirit promotes you, then every event that happens to you, good, bad, or indifferent, will lend itself to this promotion. On this basis, even that which seems bad will, in the end, turn out to bless you. Every event, whether good or bad by human judgment, can from the standpoint of spiritual judgment be made an asset. "Think of truth and not of Socrates." Let it be.